Your Child and
MONEY

A Family Activity Book

Your Child and MONEY

A Family Activity Book

Adapted from materials by

LARRY BURKETT

with **Rick Osborne**
and **Marnie Wooding**

Illustrated by **Ken Save**

MOODY PRESS
CHICAGO

Larry Burkett's Money Matters for Kids™
Executive Producer: *Allen Burkett*

For Lightwave
Managing Editor: *Elaine Osborne*
Text Director: *K. Christie Bowler*
Art Director: *Terry Van Roon*
Desktop: *Andrew Jaster*

ISBN: 0-8024-3149-6

Printed in the United States of America

The Approach

Chapter One

Getting Started

In the Middle of Life

Life gets frantic. There are so many things to do, plan, and start, so many activities to chauffeur the kids to, pay fees for, and organize. How can you find the time and energy to teach your children all they should know, show your love, discipline wisely, oversee manners, and assist them to master batting, obedience, and wise shopping? The task is daunting. But, with a little preparation, the answer is straightforward: Teach and train your children right in the middle of doing, overseeing, and running errands! Effective training is a matter of mind-set and attitude. It's as simple as 1 – 2 – 3 – 4: (1) Understand the topic; (2) Live out your understanding; (3) Communicate the topic; (4) Help with application. All of this happens right in the middle of life. That's great, because life is exactly what you're teaching.

The training steps overlap. When your lives are an open book to your children, their learning will happen with yours. For example: You learn about budgeting. Your children know that and ask questions. You explain what you're learning and why. They watch you put it into practice and try to emulate you. Then, as they ask for money and as you go shopping or pay bills, you speak naturally about how it affects your budget. Budgeting becomes a topic at church, the store, the supper table, the gas station, and more.

Two-Part Learning

No one can learn anything practical through *teaching* alone. Would you trust a dentist who had only read books? A dentist must know how teeth are made, the location of the nerves, and the various treatments available. A doctor must know how the body works and responds to illness and drugs. A Christian must know the Bible and understand basic theology, such as Jesus' divinity and humanity. But that's not enough.

The other crucial part of learning is *training:* the hands-on application of what is learned. The dentist must practice taking X rays and doing fillings. The surgeon must practice cutting and suturing. And Christians must apply their knowledge of God's Word to their lives. Otherwise, the knowledge is purposeless. Why teach children the importance of a clean room unless they know how to keep it clean? They must also learn how to fold clothes, use a vacuum, and make a bed. Teaching and training are best done *together*. That happens in life as teachable, trainable moments present themselves.

Seize the Moment

In the middle of your responsibilities and commitments, planning times to impart knowledge and train in application seems like one more pressure. Not so. Life is happening all around you whether you plan it or not. And every life event is a ready-made opportunity to teach and train your children. Be ready to grab those opportunities. The key is recognizing the moment. God referred to this when He told the Israelites to use every part of life to teach their children (Deuteronomy 6:7–9).

Some of the best times to train come when your children ask questions or are dealing with problems and their interest is high. Don't try to teach wise spending in the middle of a ball game. When children ask questions, they're primed to learn. A couple minutes of solid teaching at that moment will stay with them longer than six lectures. Use their interest and curiosity.

God is good at using life's circumstances to teach and grow you. He'll do the same for your children. His heart is that they learn to apply His principles to everyday life so they'll have the best possible life. Be on the lookout for that God-given opportunity where teaching and training collide to create a real-life teachable, trainable moment.

They're Watching!

Modeling is another way to teach and train children. Children love and look up to their parents. God designed it that way. They watch what you do in tough and good times. Don't think you can teach something only if

you've mastered it. Watching you learn is a great training tool. Children listen to how you talk about work, other people, and problems. They notice your responses to temptation, frustration, windfalls, and shortages. They know more about your honesty, diligence, and money handling than you realize. Do they watch you keep that extra change or gossip about a colleague? Or do they see you return the change, pray for that colleague, or work extra hours without grumbling? Whatever you're doing, they're learning. Guaranteed.

The key is to make sure they're seeing you do what you want them to do. You're the one they pattern themselves after. Your fears and small dishonesties become theirs. In the same way, your good money management, positive attitudes, trust, and diligence become theirs. Use their attentiveness to your life for their benefit. And remember: You don't have to be perfect. God's grace is bigger than your failures. When you blow it, simply admit your mistake and let them see you ask God and others to forgive you—then make it right and grow from it. That shows it's OK for *them* to make mistakes and learn. In fact, growing together in God's grace is the most effective learning possible. You can say, "I'm trusting God to teach me. Let's trust Him together for that." It's an excellent opportunity to pray together, asking for wisdom and help.

Using This Book

Why This Book?

Although effective teaching and training happen in the middle of life, some preparation is needed. You can't grab the moment if you don't have the information ready. Each chapter in this book is designed to help you be ready.

At times we'll encourage you to plan a teachable moment. You can "seed" life and purposely set up opportunities with a few props, actions, or words. These times can be just as effective as spontaneous ones.

Topic:

We briefly explain the basic biblical teaching on a topic. Much of this might be familiar, but if it's new, take the time to read and understand it. We've organized the teaching in a logical progression to give you a clear grasp of the main points your children will need to learn. Our goal is to enable you to easily and clearly explain the topic in a variety of contexts.

Places to Model It:

Once you've grasped the information, you'll apply it to your own life as your children watch. We give examples of how, where, and when you can live out the material. There are as many different times as there are people. Our goal is to help you see the opportunities present in your everyday life and how you might use them.

Tips to Teach It:

This is the heart of the book. We give examples of situations where the chapter's topic can be effectively taught. Some situations can be created with minimal planning. Our goal is for these tips to focus your attention on the myriad opportunities available in your child's life. The situations described are a starting place. Once you're thinking that way, you'll find many others.

Tools to Do It:

We give a key Bible verse for your kids to memorize to keep the chapter's teaching in their head and heart. (If you know the verse, it will be easy, in the middle of a conversation or activity, to help them learn it.) We also provide a variety of tools to drive the point home. These include outings, games, forms, fridge reminders, Bible stories, lists, and other resources. When you've used an opportunity life has provided to get into a topic and have laid the foundation, pull out some of these tools to reinforce and expand the teaching.

Trivia and Jokes:

We have scattered fun and interesting jokes and trivia throughout this book. These can be used as discussion starters or just for fun.

Motto:

We provide mottos to help reinforce each chapter's topic. You can use the mottos we suggest or make some up on your own that are unique to your family.

What to Do

With a little preparation you'll be ready to take advantage of the moments God provides.

- Go over the theory until it's clear in your mind.

- Take a look at the modeling examples. Think of other times and places you can use.

- Read the tips carefully, and you'll recognize opportunities as they arise. Trust God to show you when you're in the middle of a teachable moment.

- Become familiar with the tools. Learn how the games work and review the Bible stories. Be sure you can explain the forms simply.

- Finally, pray for God's help in recognizing opportunities, communicating His principles, and making the teaching practical.

Who's in Charge?

Topic

What Is Stewardship?

Stewardship simply means that God made and owns everything, and He gives us things to look after. We're His managers. We need to learn to care for what He gives us in the way He sets it out in the Bible. We'll find that when we do things God's way, life works out best for us and God will trust us with more. There are at least seven different items or kinds of things that we are stewards of. (We'll explain each item in greater detail later in the chapter.)

Your Relationship with God: Openly seek God in all things (Philippians 3:14).

Your Relationship with Others: Strive for mutual love and respect (1 John 3:23).

Who You Are: Love and care for yourself (Philippians 4:8; 1 Peter 3:3–4).

What You Choose: Submit your will to God's will and make right choices (Matthew 16:24–25).

What You Do with Your Time: Manage your time wisely (Matthew 25:1–13).

What You Own: Be responsible and generous with your possessions (2 Corinthians 9:6–8).

What You Are Able to Do: Use your gifts and talents for God (Romans 12:1–8).

JOKE

Why is the moon like a dollar?

Because it has four quarters.

Stewardship Is the Start

To help your children understand that they are stewards of everything they have—including time, talents, and material resources—here are some things they'll need to know:

God owns everything. He designed and made it all. You might say God has the ultimate copyright. *"The earth belongs to the Lord. And so does everything in it"* (Psalm 24:1).

God gave it all to us. Why? Because He loves us. Everything around us is a gift for us to use and enjoy. *"Every good and perfect gift is from God. It comes down from the Father. He created the heavenly lights. He does not change like shadows that move"* (James 1:17).

We are God's stewards. God's immense care package comes to us with the responsibility to take care of our things in the way God instructs us. A good steward manages God's gifts—from the world around us, to the people we love, our jobs, our talents, and the objects in our home—with respect, responsibility, and an understanding of the truths in the Bible. *"Much will be required of everyone who has been given much. Even more will be asked of the person who is supposed to take care of much"* (Luke 12:48).

The Bible is our guide. The Bible gives us principles that teach us how to be good stewards, and how to be faithful, wise, generous, and thankful in how we use what God gives us.

Doing things God's way brings us joy and peace. When we follow God's principles, pray for His guidance, and trust Him to provide for us, we become living examples of the way He designed the world to work. As we become good stewards, God entrusts us with more to manage for Him, as did the master with the faithful steward in the story Jesus told. *"The second servant came to his master. He said, 'Sir, your money has earned five times as much.' His master answered, 'I will put you in charge of five towns'"* (Luke 19:18–19).

Places to Model It!

Let's look more closely at the things we are stewards of and see how you can model stewardship for your children.

Your Relationship with God:

Follow Him. Be somebody who openly seeks God's love, Word, and guidance. Let your children see you having regular "one-on-one" times with God. Tell them how much you enjoy these times and the benefits you get from them. Remember to thank and honor God always. That's the best example of all.

Your Relationship with Others:

Love one another. Relationships are one of God's greatest blessings for us. As we love others, we too are loved. In our relationships we should look for what we can do for others, rather than for how we can serve ourselves. That's the kind

TRIVIA

How long can a coin's life span be? *Thousands of years.*

of relationship God has with us. He's generous, caring, and giving. Your children will have healthy relationships in the future by seeing how you care for people today. Be an illustration of God's heart by loving, giving, forgiving, and supporting others. Show your children that God's way of treating others is the best way.

Who You Are:

Love yourself. God loves us unconditionally and has made each of us unique and special. He wants us to like who we are and to take good care of ourselves. That means eating well, exercising, having good hygiene, and doing things that support a healthy self-image. Our children learn about proper self-esteem partly by seeing their parents' positive attitude about themselves.

What You Choose:

Choose God. God wants what is best for us. Therefore, doing things His way makes sense. God respects your choices because He loves you. To show your respect for God, lay down your will in order to follow His plan for your life. Demonstrate to your children that God's will is your will by turning off that ungodly movie or program. Read the Bible with your children. Pray as a family about important family issues and decisions. Set a positive example in your own personal behavior, activities, purchases, and entertainment choices.

What You Do with Your Time:

The meter is running. Time is God's gift to us. Using time the way God wants means maintaining a proper mix between time spent with God, family, and work. Don't make God or your family an afterthought by spending fifteen hours a day at the office. Does your life have balance? Children learn about priorities by watching you prioritize.

What You Own:

Handle with care. It's your job to faithfully manage what God has given to you. God has given generously to each of us. Being responsible in all these areas takes commitment, dedication, balance, and above all, faith in God's guidance.

TRIVIA

What is the sun's diameter?

864,000 miles.

Pray with your children for wisdom in handling these things. God wants us to be thankful for His provision and gifts. Be eager, ready, and willing to share your abundance with others. You can take care of that new car, but don't forget to use it to help others—be a parent driver for school outings, or take a senior on a pleasant Sunday drive in the country.

What You Are Able to Do:

Just do it (for Him). We all have abilities that serve our spiritual, family, and work lives. These abilities are gifts from God and are perfectly suited to who we are and to God's plan for us. Show your children that you want to give your talents back to God by using them to teach Sunday school, sing in the choir, or organize a charity event. Strive for professional excellence in all things, and be open to using your gifts in new ways. Also, share the obstacles you face, your successes, and your dedication with your children. Your trust and faith in God will be the seed that helps their trust flourish.

Tips to Teach It!

Key Verse

Help your children memorize this verse, and make sure they understand what it means.

> **"The earth belongs to the Lord. And so does everything in it."** (Psalm 24:1)

Key Bible Story

Read through Luke 19:12–26 with your children. It's the parable of the faithful steward. In this story, the stewards who were trustworthy in small matters were trusted with larger matters. Help your children apply this lesson to their lives by encouraging discussion.

- What "talents" do they have that God wants them to use wisely?

- What is the benefit of doing this?

Teachable Moments

The normal course of life is full of opportunities to draw your children's attention to the matter of stewardship. Here are some moments when you can teach the various areas of stewardship to your children. Keep an eye out for more.

Your Relationship wiyh God:

- When your child has questions about different churches and their different ways of expressing their devotion to God, talk about issues like: Christian denominations and the various ways we worship God; God's call to unity in Him, even though we are all different; and how to have a personal devotional time with God.

Your Relationship with Others:

- Take time out with your children to do special things for other people. Call on a sick friend or help out a charity function. These activities are the foundation of generous adults.

- When your children are troubled by a concern or problem, encourage them to pray about it, and ask you to pray with them. Show them that whether their concern is about school, relationships, bullies, or getting eyeglasses, you and God take it seriously.

- If your children are having problems with a friend or sibling, encourage them to talk to you about it. Explore what the Bible has to say on the issue. Pray for God's guidance, and talk about ways to resolve the problem—perhaps through apologies, forgiveness, or mediation.

- Have your child join you in doing something special for your spouse. Whether it's serving breakfast in bed or sneaking out and buying some flowers or another small gift, your child will see that your spouse is important to you.

Who You Are:

- At the video store, talk about making right choices about what you fill your mind with. For example, explain why it's not good to expose ourselves to violence.

JOKE

Why was Adam the best runner of all time?
Because he was first in the human race.

MOTTO

Be a good steward

for God!

- When your children are combing their hair, picking out clothes, or doing sports and other physical activities, discuss how wonderfully made they are, and how it is important to keep healthy and feeling good about themselves.

- On your next walk, point out boundaries such as fences and walls. Tell your children that a gardener need only take care of the area enclosed by his fence. He doesn't have to weed anyone else's garden. In the same way, we need boundaries so we don't wear ourselves out trying to care for too much. Our "fence" is ourselves. We're responsible for everything inside our skin, including our emotions, thoughts, and feelings.

What You Choose:

- When your children do something without being asked, or they work exceptionally hard on a school project, praise them, and reward them by doing something fun together. Remember: success isn't the issue, it is the desire to do what's right.

What You Do with Your Time:

- When your children find it difficult to prioritize activities and get their homework or chores done, or when play seems to be taking priority over homework, talk to your children about strategies they can use to manage their time wisely. Perhaps they can set aside an hour for play and then do homework, or, better yet, do homework first and then play. Help them create systems to make caring for things consistent and easy. For example, they could make a time schedule, a priority list, or a completed job checklist for chores or homework. Say every afternoon at three o'clock they walk the dog, or perhaps they must clean their rooms on Saturday mornings before they can play. Decide together on appropriate consequences if this priority list is violated so everybody is clear on the issues. Don't forget to follow through on all decisions.

What You Own:

- When your children receive a new pet or a new item, such as a bike, show them how to take care of their new gift. Explain that the more responsibility they display with this item, the more freedom, trust, and responsibility you will be able to give them with other things in the future. That's the way God made things to work.

- Toys in the driveway or bikes left out overnight are chances to talk about caring for our possessions. Have your children do a toy spot check at the end of the day before going inside. Perhaps you can paint a toy or bike parking spot in the garage and write their names on it, just like you may have at the office.

- When there's one cookie remaining in the cookie jar, discuss God's generosity and show your children how it is better to give than to take.

- When your children get money for allowance, chores, or as a gift, take time to talk to your children about dividing up their money God's way. Teach them to have a generous heart, and to give the first part back to God. Help them develop a budget for their money.

- The next time you hand out treats, explain that even though *you* purchased the ice cream or cookies, you want to share these good gifts with *them*. Stress that you don't have to, you want to—just like God wants to share His things with us.

What You Are Able to Do:

- Let your children try new activities—like drama or basketball—to help them explore their talents and abilities. Assist them in using these experiences to find out what they're good at, and help them understand that not everything can be mastered overnight.

- Are your children taking on the responsibility of a hobby or a musical instrument? Encourage them to pray for motivation and support during low times, and to have faith that God will use their successes and victories to reveal His plan for their lives. Show them that when we use our talents in new ways we become encouraged, confident, and excited about doing more.

TRIVIA

What did Adam and Eve make clothes out of?

Fig leaves.

Tools to Do It!

1 Take a walk through the park. Talk about God's creation and what a wonderful gift it is. Take trash bags with you and pick up any garbage you find as a way to demonstrate good stewardship.

2 Get your children involved in your recycling program. Explain to them that we are stewards of our world.

3 Hold a contest with a prize for the child that can take care of his or her room for the longest period of time without being asked.

4 Help your children make a priority list of their daily activities. Compare that list with your own. Talk about how they are different or the same.

5 Use a calendar on the fridge or other special place to schedule time to pray together, do a Bible study, have fun, and do chores together. Make these dates a priority in your life. Each day, have your children write out on a calendar one way that God has blessed them. Compare and discuss lists at the end of each week.

6 Photocopy the calligraphied stewardship list provided on the next page (or cut out the one in the back of the book) and place it on your fridge or bulletin board. Your children can draw pictures explaining what each one of the items means to them.

7 Play the twenty questions game. Have someone think of an object God has given them to care for. Get the other players to try and guess the answer using less than twenty questions that can only be answered by "yes" or "no."

8 Look at the following verses as a family or with each child separately: Luke 12:20–21; Psalm 147:4–5; James 1:25; and Psalm 139:14. Read the context and discuss what part of stewardship the verse is talking about, what it means, and how it applies to our lives here and now.

TRIVIA

What are the first three words in the Old Testament?

"In the beginning."

Follow God

Openly seek God in all things (Philippians 3:14).

Love One Another

Strive for mutual love and respect (1 John 3:23).

Love Yourself

Love and care for yourself (Philippians 4:8; 1 Peter 3:3–4).

Choose God

Submit your will to God's will and make right choices (Matthew 16:24–25).

The Meter is Running

Manage your time wisely (Matthew 25:1–13).

Handle With Care

Be responsible and generous with your possessions (2 Corinthians 9:6–8).

Just Do It (for God)

Use your gifts and talents for God (Romans 12:1–8)

Chapter Three

In God We Trust

Topic

What Is Trust?

When we trust God we rely on Him to care for us. God is everywhere, He understands everything, He can do anything, and He can perfectly provide for our needs. The more we know about God's character and love, the more we will trust Him in all things.

The Trusting Kind

Our society puts a great deal of emphasis on self-reliance. Somehow, in our struggle to be independent, we view trust as a weakness, not a strength. But the act of trusting God strengthens our faith, our confidence, and our families.

God loves us. He is in control of everything, He knows what is best for us, and He will provide for all our needs. No situation is too big for God. He has a plan for our lives that surpasses anything that we could ever envision for ourselves. God's love is unchanging, eternal, and totally trustworthy.

To trust God means to put aside our fears and place our present and our future squarely into His hands. Trust is part of a deeper understanding of His love and care for us. Learning about God's love frees us from worry, so we can face life's challenges with confidence. Trusting God doesn't mean there won't be trouble spots and obstacles in our lives, but it does mean that God is with us each step of the way.

The right road is to trust God and the people He puts into our lives to care for us. When we allow God to work in our lives we can do our jobs better, our money matters improve, and our relationships are more fulfilling. We become the type of people that our world is looking for: the trusting kind. *"May the God who gives hope fill you with great joy. May you have perfect peace as you trust in him. May the power of the Holy Spirit fill you with hope"* (Romans 15:13).

Places to Model It!

Your children trust you, as a parent, to teach them the right things. Use their trust in you to teach them how to trust in God. How do you react when trouble strikes? Do car repairs put you in a tailspin, or get you seeking God for provision? Let your children see that discomfort doesn't make you distrustful of God. Trouble doesn't change God. His love is as solid as ever. Demonstrate trust in action—seek God's guidance through prayer, Bible study, and counsel from other godly adults.

QUOTE

Jesus said we should never worry about what will happen tomorrow.

RIDDLE

Which side of an American quarter has the motto "In God we trust"? *Heads.*

Tips to Teach It!

Key Verse

"May the God who gives hope fill you with great joy. May you have perfect peace as you trust in him. May the power of the Holy Spirit fill you with hope." (Romans 15:13)

Key Bible Story

The story of the loaves and fishes (Matthew 15:32–38) is a great illustration of how God provides for all of our needs. Read through the story with your children and highlight God's power and provision. Ask them:

- If God can do this, what else is He able to do?

- What does the story tell us about how God can care for us?

Teachable Moments

Trust is more than an action—it's a lifestyle. Here are some examples of the different ways we trust God:

Trusting God's Care:

- When you go to the grocery store, talk to your children about how you trust the people at the store to supply you with good food that won't make you sick. In the same way, God is the expert on what we need to live good, healthy lives. He knows the best time to give us certain things in our lives.

- When your children show they trust you, tell them that they need to trust God in the same way. Tell them that, just like you, God wants to love them, provide for them, keep them healthy and happy, be there when they have problems, and give them clothes, food, and a home. Just like you, God wants them to have the best life possible.

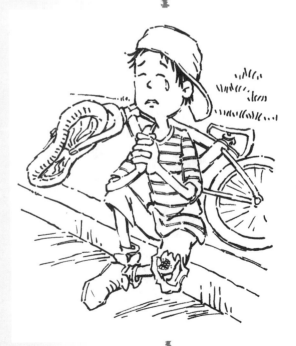

Trusting God's Love:

- When you groom your pet, clean its cage, or take it out for exercise, talk with your child about how your family loves the pet and how you all provide for its health and happiness. Have your child think of the many ways your pet loves and trusts the family members. Compare this with the way we should trust and depend on God.

- Does your teen crave thrills like bungee jumping? When your children talk about their desire to do such activities, use the moment to compare trust in God with the trust one must have in the bungee cord and the people who supervise the jump. Show them how parents and pastors are like a bungee support team. They prepare us to leap into a trusting relationship with God. But remind them that to decide to trust and commit oneself to God is an individual choice. The bungee cord that connects us to God is our trust, and the structure that the cord is connected to is God's love and commitment. But, unlike bungee cords, trust in God is one hundred percent reliable.

- When God answers one of your children's prayers, draw his or her attention to that fact. Use the event to show them that God heard them and responded.

Trusting God's Provision:

- If your children want to purchase something, go to summer camp, or go on a class trip, but don't have the money yet, sit down and talk with them about the feasibility of obtaining that goal. Review their financial situation, and help them come up with plans to achieve their goals. Pray with them about their situation. Children need to learn that money matters shouldn't be separate from their daily walk with God. Good stewardship of their money is part of trusting in God's provision and plan for them.

Trusting God's Control

When big decisions or problems confront you individually or as a family, demonstrate your trust in God's guidance and his ability to control the situation. Seek God's wisdom, and when the event or

TRIVIA

How many colors does the rainbow have?

Six. In order, they are violet, blue, green, yellow, orange, and red. Sometimes indigo is included in the list.

WALKMAN

decision is resolved, talk about what happened, what God did, and how you made your decision.

Trusting God's Design:

- While driving your children to art class or swimming lessons, discuss their abilities, talents, and interests. Encourage them to pray that God would reveal His plan for their lives. Be a voice of trusting experience and an example of trust in action. Show them that "In God we trust" should also mean "In God we find peace."

Trusting in God's Right Outcome:

- When a teen starts baby-sitting, review safety rules with them. Explain that these rules are not in place to spoil the child's fun, but to protect the child from harm. Sometimes saying "no" to a child is a necessity. As parents, you want to give your children what they want or need whenever you feel it is right. God also wants to give them what they want and need. Tell your children that sometimes God has to say "no" to us for our own good. We may trust God and ask Him for certain things, but that doesn't mean He will always give them to us. He uses His judgment to keep us safe from harm, and to help us have a good life. Teach your children that it is up to us to respect both God's "no," and His "yes" in our lives.

TRIVIA

How old was Joseph when he was sold into slavery? *Seventeen (Genesis 37:2).*

Tools to Do It!

1 Play the "Trust Me" game. This game takes two people. One person stands behind the other, ready to catch the first person as he or she falls backwards into the second person's arms. This is a simple game, but it takes responsibility and care on one hand (to actually catch the falling person), and trust on the other (believing that you will be caught). Try it in a group with different combina-

tions of players. Use the game to explain that trust is both a choice and an action.

2 Children often think that miracles don't happen anymore. Take time to point out that though many present-day miracles may be easy to explain in modern terms, they are still evidence of God's care in our lives. For instance, when a sailor is swept out to sea, and a day later he is found, still alive, that's a miracle! Explain that even though our lives may seem easier than those of Joseph or Moses, we still have to trust and obey God in the same way as these great leaders in the Bible. God is just as faithful to us as He was to them.

3 There are a number of great Bible illustrations of God's faithfulness and the need for us to trust in Him. Take a look at these verses as a family, and see how they apply to your own life: Matthew 6:25–34; Matthew 17:24–27; Daniel 3:16–30; and Exodus 14 & 16.

MOTTO

Try Trusting God—

it works!

Giving Is Living

Chapter Four

Topic

Live to Give; Give to Live

Generosity, giving, and tithing are simple concepts to explain to children. God is incredibly generous with us—He gives us food, clothing, shelter, families, friends, pets, and so many other good things. In gratitude we should give something back to Him. We can do this by giving, or tithing, to the church, helping others, or just being generous with our love, money, time, and abilities. We should share God's goodness with an open hand and a joyful heart.

Generosity, Giving, and Tithing in Our Lives

It is important for children to know where generosity comes from, and why it is a positive quality. Explain that it begins with God, whose character is the epitome of generosity. We know this because He has given us everything we need to live. Generosity is a characteristic that we should display in our own lives through the acts of tithing and giving. Being generous means taking the "me" out of our daily thoughts and lives and replacing it with "others." Here is how generosity works:

God is good and generous to us. He provides everything we need and more. He loves to give to us. We should pass on God's generosity to others. Giving to and caring for others is a witness to how well we are cared for by God. Sometimes God gives us an excess so we can share His joy in giving with others. Generosity should be a joyous celebration, and an important part of our daily lives. We become effective givers by wisely giving where and when God directs. When we start to value and love people more than money and desires, we demonstrate that we value the same things that God treasures. *"Your heart will be where your riches are"* (Luke 12:34).

Tithing is giving God the first part of what He has given us. The word tithe means one-tenth. That means one-tenth of what we earn or receive should go to God's work in the world through the local church and through missions. This is how God planned for us to provide financial support for His work. Tithing is an outward act that displays our thankful hearts and our belief that everything belongs to God. *"Honor the Lord with your wealth. Give him the first share of all your crops. Then your storerooms will be so full they can't hold everything. Your huge jars will spill over with fresh wine"* (Proverbs 3:9–10). We can also tithe our time, abilities, and talents.

TRIVIA

How do you spell tithe?

*A **T**enth **I**n **T**hanks to **H**im for **E**verything.*

TRIVIA

How many people did Jesus feed with five loaves of bread and three fish?

Five thousand.

30

The amount of time, energy, or money we give is not the issue with God; He is concerned with our attitude. God loves a cheerful giver. *"Here is something to remember. The one who plants only a little will gather only a little. And the one who plants a lot will gather a lot. You should each give what you have decided in your heart to give. You shouldn't give if you don't want to. You shouldn't give because you are forced to. God loves a cheerful giver"* (2 Corinthians 9:6–7). Being a cheerful giver is our way of saying thank you to God.

When we trust God, we are free to be the generous givers that God intended. Financial worries can be a stumbling block to our generosity. We worry we don't have enough money, energy, or time to do the things we want to do. Jesus taught that we should *"put God's kingdom first. Do what he wants you to do. Then all of those things will also be given to [us]"* (Matthew 6:33).

By trusting God to take care of us, we are free to give to others. Helping others will change how we use our money and time, and, most importantly, how we look at life. When we give generously and obediently, we show God that we trust Him. God responds by providing for our needs, whether by giving us more, or showing us how to live on less. We can never out-give God, but we can help others where and when God wants us to.

Places to Model It!

Modeling generosity is a matter of keeping our eyes open to God's opportunities to give of ourselves and our resources. Here are some helpful tips:

- Model an attitude of thankfulness at all times. Show that you recognize that God is your provider. For example, when you are shopping, give a quick thank you to God for helping you get a good deal on your purchases. Also, make sure your kids hear you verbally thank people—from clerks, to neighbors, to family members.

MOTTO

Live to give;

give to live.

- Get your children involved in your giving activities. Demonstrate little acts of generosity in your daily life, like helping an elderly lady with her bags, stopping to help a lost child in the mall, or being a sponsor for a charity event. Discuss how good it feels to give to others. Show your children that giving is, in a very real sense, receiving.

- When you give your time and money to the church or a charity, set the giving attitude. Be honest with your children. Let them know that giving isn't always easy, but it demonstrates that you value what God values. Show them how generosity leads to positive relationships, a good reputation, and self-confidence. When tithing or donating your time, talents, abilities, and experience, do it wholeheartedly and with enthusiasm. Always show respect to the recipients of your help.

Tips to Teach It!

Key Verse

Explain that this verse tells us to put God first. He'll take care of the rest.

> *"Honor the Lord with your wealth. Give him the first share of all your crops. Then your storerooms will be so full they can't hold everything. Your huge jars will spill over with fresh wine."* (Proverbs 3:9–10)

Key Bible Story

Together with your children, take a look at the first tithe when Abraham gave a tenth of his belongings to Melchizedek out of gratitude to God (Genesis 14:8–24).

- Did Abraham have to give Melchizedek a tenth of his belongings?

- Why did he do it?

Teachable Moments

Take the following opportunities in your everyday life to teach your children about tithing, generosity, and giving.

Tithing:

- When your children are old enough to receive a regular allowance or income, talk about their responsibility to give the first part back to God. Be open about your tithing. Talk about why you do it, how it makes you feel, and the good things that happen because you give your money and time. Take them to church and show them all the things their tithe provides.

Giving:

- If your child sees an opportunity to give, do charity work, or be a "Good Samaritan," encourage him or her to discuss it with you and get involved. You can make advice, supervision, or driving part of your contribution. Generosity is a habit you can give to your kids—a godly, learned behavior.

- Help your children explore their abilities and talents and encourage them to think about where and when they can use them to help others. Perhaps they could pass out cookies at the next church event, play music at a party, or baby-sit for parents who are attending a meeting.

- If your children want to donate money to charities in other countries, explain how our dollar, which only buys a soft

QUOTE

King David wrote, "The Lord is my Shepherd; I shall not want" (Psalm 23 KJV).

drink here, can buy clothes, medicine, and much more in poorer countries. It doesn't take much money, by our standards, to change someone else's world.

Generosity:

- There will be times when your children find giving difficult. When you are sorting through old toys or clothes, often there are items that your children don't use anymore, but that they find difficult to give away. Point out how happy that toy will make another little girl or boy. Together, you can clean and prepare the items for donation. Your children will feel good about putting God's words into action in this tangible way.

- When the last candy rattles around the jar, or it's time to let someone else have a turn on the video game, or that hard-earned dollar is going into the collection plate, help your children understand that giving to others is important, even if it stings a little. Teach them that we don't have to be afraid to give. God loves us and will provide all we need. There'll be another candy, another game, and another dollar to spend.

- Every time you and your children give, pray a celebration prayer thanking God for His provision, blessing, and care. Thank Him for the church, your opportunity to be a part of it, and the opportunity to help others.

- Your children can be great witnesses for their friends by being people who can be turned to during times of need. If the gang is going to the movies but one friend doesn't have the money, encourage your child to treat that friend to a show. Time and skills can also be shared. Perhaps your child has a skill like sewing or bike repair. Encourage him or her to help a friend make a dress, fix a bike, or do chores.

Tools to Do It!

1 As a family, adopt a missionary family or a child in need overseas, and pledge a certain amount per week or month. Let your children help send off the donation. Have them research the country and people where your money is going. Have a dinner that features the traditional food of that culture, or have the family write letters to their adopted friends.

2 Two great places to obtain information about charitable organizations are the Evangelical Council for Financial Accountability at PO Box 17456, Washington, DC, 20041–0456. Web address: http://www.sim.org/ecfa/ or the Interdenominational Foreign Mission Association of North America, PO Box 398, Wheaton, IL 60189–0398. Web address: http://www.sim.org/ifma

3 Help your children organize their own giving jars for their tithe and other charities. Assist them in dividing their allowance or employment money into the right jars or envelopes. Make tithing smooth by helping with the math and supplying change if they need it to make the money division easy and clear.

4 Encourage your children to empty their tithing jar or envelope at a set time each week, and take the money to the church. To make it a fun family affair, plan a giving dinner or a treat to celebrate God's blessings. Choose a special meal, a great dessert, and a favorite board game to play after the meal.

5 Tell your children about the needs in your community. Take them to the local food bank to help out. Point needs and needy people out to them when you see them. It's important to expose our children to the needs around them.

6 Your children, along with the church youth group or with friends, can organize their own event that will raise money for a charity of their choice, with your approval. Giving doesn't have to be as boring as writing a check. It can be a fun way to get something that can be a witness to others.

7 Solve the mystery of the disappearing tithe money by taking your children on a field trip to your church and showing them what their money is used

JOKE

How many fish does it take to serve ten people? *None, fish aren't very good at serving. Better do it yourself.*

for. A good project could be to make a list of how the money is used. Here are some examples:

- Building: rent or mortgage
- Building: heat and light
- Phone
- Office equipment—like computers, photocopiers, and fax machines
- Postage
- Office and Sunday school supplies
- Pastors' and other staff salaries
- Missions and other ministries
- Building and grounds maintenance
- Advertising
- Special events
- Lighting and sound equipment

8 Have your children tape interviews with individuals and ask them questions about their job, programs, or volunteer work at the church.

9 Take a look at the following Bible verses as a family, and discuss why tithing, giving, and generosity were as important then as they are now: Genesis 28:10–22; Mark 12:42–44; Luke 10:30–37.

JOKE

Why are missionaries like tennis players?

They both love to serve.

Enough Is Enough

Topic

Contentment and Diligence: What Are They?

You can explain this concept to your children by telling them that contentment is being at peace with our financial and overall life situation. It comes down to trusting that God is in control—He takes care of us and provides for all of our needs. Diligence is trying to do the best job we can at everything we do, and viewing everything we do as being done directly for God.

Contentment and Diligence: Partners in Peace

Our part of contented living is following God's plan for our lives, and being willing to do the things He asks of us, trusting in His care and protection. Here are the main points your children should know about contentment and diligence:

- *God loves us*. We can trust Him to know and care for all of our needs and desires. *"Don't be controlled by love for money. Be happy with what you have. God has said, 'I will never leave you. I will never desert you'"* (Hebrews 13:5). The bottom line is that God is here for us every day of our lives, and He wants to provide for us in every way: spiritually, emotionally, financially, practically, and physically. If we truly need something, God will supply it. That's something we can count on.

- *Contentment is priceless*. Many people think that a certain amount of money or type of house, car, boat, vacation, education, job, etc., will make them happy. But this type of thinking leads to discontentment and dissatisfaction, and it ultimately distracts us from our relationship with God. Contentment isn't about how much or how little we have; contentment is about following God's direction and timing in our lives. When we do this, we will live joyful, productive, peaceful lives. We will be secure and at peace.

MOTTO

Don't just do it,
do it right.

38

- *God is the creator of excellence*. Therefore, mediocrity should have no place in our lives. In all our pursuits and relationships we should diligently pursue excellence and do everything as if we're doing it for the Lord. *"Work at everything you do with all your heart. Work as if you were working for the Lord, not for human masters"* (Colossians 3:23).

- *Diligence is a witness to others*. God's way of diligence doesn't just get us from point A to point B by the fastest route possible. His diligence helps us pick up certain character traits along the way that we can use and build upon. These traits include self-respect, discipline, confidence, an eye for excellence, and a desire to please God. These are the character traits that the world is looking for. *"Do you see people who do good work? They will serve kings. They won't serve ordinary people"* (Proverbs 22:29). People will trust, respect, and want to work with the person who is diligent in all the things God has set before him or her. In short, when we do our best for God, it benefits us by building us a solid reputation and good relationships.

Places to Model It!

Modeling contentment and diligence involves living a joyful life based on God's Word. The following points are a few suggestions on how to show your children the "good" life.

Contentment:
- Contentment isn't something you find; it's something you make. You can create contentment by small daily changes of perspective or attitude. When negative feelings start to creep into your thoughts, stop, think, thank, pray, and continue on.

- Everybody has those "Monday" days when they have to work late or the mechanic won't have the car ready on time. These are the times to stop and think about what you are saying or what kind of attitude you are displaying to your children. If you feel you aren't conveying the message you want to convey, rethink the situation and thank God for the good things about the situation or person. Remind yourself of God's patience, love, and care for you, and then pray about how you can be a positive influence. This mental change of gears can turn a negative into a positive, and lead to uplifting results and responses.

- Show your children how to be constructive and positive changers when it comes to situations with their relationships, job, finances, and fellow Christians.

- Do the same for those little annoying things that for some strange reason really get you hopping, like broken dishes, paper cuts, and gum on your shoes. It's helpful to discuss your own change in attitude or emotions with your children. Let them know your process of attitude switching. Contentment is a continuing process of adjusting our attitude by trusting God's way.

Diligence:

- The most effective way to teach diligence is to show your children excellence in action. When you work diligently and successfully at your jobs, be it at home or at the office, you show your children an effective way of conducting their lives.

- Let them see your diligence on a daily basis. Be reliable, punctual, and don't cut corners on excellence. Work hard at your relationships with family and friends. This teaches your children about commitment. You want to teach them about good friendships, promise-keeping, and respecting each other in all situations.

JOKE

Why couldn't the orange finish the race?

It ran out of juice.

Tips to Teach It!

Key Verses

Help your kids memorize these two key verses on contentment and diligence and talk about what they mean.

Contentment:

> **"Don't be controlled by love for money. Be happy with what you have. God has said, 'I will never leave you. I will never desert you.'" (Hebrews 13:5)**

Diligence:

> **"Work at everything you do with all your heart. Work as if you were working for the Lord, not for human masters." (Colossians 3:23)**

Key Bible Stories

Read through the following Bible passages with your children and then use the accompanying questions to guide a short discussion.

Contentment:

Paul's feelings of perfect contentment in Christ throughout his many trials is an inspiration for today's Christians (Acts 16:22–34).

Diligence:

The story of hardworking Joseph and his rise to power in Egypt is a great model of diligence and its eventual rewards (Genesis 39–41).

- What helped Paul to be content when he had been beaten and was in jail?

- How can we be content with what we have?

Teachable Moments

Take these daily moments to teach contentment and diligence to your children.

Contentment:

- Siblings often squabble about portions of ice cream, pop, or the size of cake slices that are being divided out. When this happens, stop and discuss how this behavior takes the fun out of giving them the treat, and how it ruins the fun of receiving it.

- When your child really wants something, first help him or her to be content and thankful with what they have, and then pray about God's timing for a change or for something new.

- It will take time before your children will understand the difference between needs, wants, and desires. You can explain it to them like this: Needs are the things you require to live and to have a good life. Wants and desires are extra things that help you or entertain you. Teach your children to develop a proper balance between what they need and what they want. Tell them that God wants to give them what they want, but only if it is good for them.

Diligence:

- When you do chores with your children, make sure they do them properly. No "sweeping the dust under the rug," so to speak. Take the time to show your children how to properly use appliances, cleaning products, and other tools.

- Review your children's homework. Discuss areas which they can improve upon. Remember that it is their homework, and that their level of excellence may be different than yours.

- If a child gets a low mark on a school assignment, test, or report card, encourage him or her to talk with the teacher about what was expected. A teacher's list of requirements may help improve the assignments.

- Ask your children how they can go beyond what is expected. A little guidance in time budgeting may be helpful, too. Diligence is learning the skills and using them to do a good job on time, every time.

- Completing what you start is another part of diligence. Whether it's schoolwork, sports, music, chores, or caring for pets and toys, help your child to make a plan to stay with it, even after the novelty has worn thin.

- A parent/child contract helps define responsibilities and consequences before lessons are arranged or purchases are made. If your child doesn't meet his or her responsibilities, be prepared to follow through on the mutually-agreed-upon consequences.

Tools to Do It!

Contentment:

1 Do a media study game. Make a family night of watching a few television commercials. Talk about how they can make you feel unhappy or discontented with yourself, others, and your possessions. Ask your children how they could do the ad differently. Have them write their own commercial using positive messages about a product and why someone would need it. Act out the new commercial, or even better, videotape it and show it to family and friends. Perhaps your Sunday school could hold a commercial production contest.

2 Have your child make a list of the things God has given them and then throw a "Thank You God" party and invite some friends.

3 Discuss the desire for "in" products. Check out ads in various papers and magazines with different brands of the same product. See if the "in" brand really is that different from or better than the others. Teach your children that sometimes the most expensive brand is the best product, but at other times we just think a brand name is the best because we've been convinced by the company's marketing campaign.

TRIVIA

When were the first American dollars minted?

1794.

4. Learn about a missionary project in another country and compare what you feel is essential to your lives with what the people in that country may feel are necessities. Is there a difference? Discuss why. Encourage your children to find pen pals so they can learn about other people's lives and needs. Or, if possible, take your family on a short-term missions trip.

5. When your child out-grows his or her bike, hockey equipment, video game, or other important item, have them repair or rejuvenate the item and give it to someone who would really love to have it. They can paint and polish their old bike, or fix up their old hamster cage with new pet toys, food, and bedding to make the gift extra special.

6. Help your children plan savings goals for their spending money. But keep the goals small, so your children feel good about the progress they are making and don't get frustrated. Let them know that small deposits are just as important as large ones. Children are never too young to learn financial contentment.

Diligence:

1. Have a contest and see who can clean their room the fastest (without compromising quality). Have a checklist of requirements and standards that must be met. Give a special prize to the winner, or special prizes for certain categories, like best dust-buster, bed-maker or drawer-organizer.

2 Post a job board of household chores that you're willing to pay for. It will teach your children about individual effort for remuneration, and how the quality of their work affects their reputation:

- On a piece of 12-inch-by-18-inch cardboard write "Quality Labor Required."

- Use post-it notes to write household jobs and fair wages on. Include age limits and qualifications needed. Stick them to the board. Find jobs that go beyond the usual cleanup.

- Terms of Employment (to be posted). Photocopy the list from the next page and post it on or beside your job board. Go over the terms with your children to make sure they understand them.

Terms of Employment

1. Every job must be inspected before payment is made.

2. No partially-done job will receive payment.

3. Pray about choosing jobs. Be sure you don't take on more than you can do.

4. Management will be available to discuss qualifications and training for these jobs.

5. Age and experience are factors.

6. All jobs must be done diligently. This means you need to work hard, work quickly, and do a thorough job.

7. All regular chores must be completed before taking a job from the board.

8. Management reserves the right not to pay for slack, slow, or sloppy work.

9. Management reserves the right to pay bonuses for jobs that are exceptionally well-done (all jobs must be well-done).

10. Management pays by the job, not by the hour.

11. These terms are nonnegotiable.

Honesty Is the Best Policy

Topic

Honesty and Integrity: What Are They?

Honesty and integrity are big words for children, but their meanings are simple. Honesty means always bringing out the whole truth in what we do or say. Integrity means living out what we believe and know to be right. In other words, it's being committed to living a Christian life, and following God's laws and instructions.

Honesty and Integrity At Work in Our Lives

We don't have to look far to see that honesty and integrity are precious and often rare commodities. We can do our part to change that fact by making sure our children understand how to live out these qualities.

We are called to be honest because God is honest. The Bible tells us that God is truth and He cannot lie. If God is honest, then His creation must also reflect that quality. The Bible teaches us how things work. Honesty reflects God's heart to the world. When we are honest in our financial and personal dealings, people trust and respect us. A reputation for honesty will precede us and open doors of opportunity and friendship.

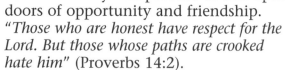

"Those who are honest have respect for the Lord. But those whose paths are crooked hate him" (Proverbs 14:2).

Integrity means being the same on the inside as we are on the outside. *"Those who live without blame walk safely. But those who take crooked paths will get caught"* (Proverbs 10:9). When we have integrity, we live out what we believe so that others can see it. We walk it and we talk it. Integrity is part of the godly system that helps us build right attitudes, good reputations, good relationships, a good witness, and a true walk with God. People want to be around a person of integrity.

Places to Model It!

Do you want to know the fastest way to model honesty? Do what you say.

Honesty:

- When you say you'll go to your child's sports game or do a chore, do it. Your family motto should be "Honesty is our only policy." Honesty makes a family a team with no secrets.

- Tell a story about a time when you were tempted to be dishonest. If you gave in to temptation, you can explain what happened as a result. How did it make you feel? What were the consequences? How did you set it right, or can you make it right, right now? If you resisted the temptation, tell your children how and why things worked out.

Integrity:

- Children have a keen eye for integrity, so it is important for you to live out what you say you believe. Instruct your children in what the Bible tells us is right, then do what the Bible says. Be a godly role model for your kids, and show them how honesty and integrity can improve their life, reputation, and relationships. You can do this by investing in products that reflect your values, by acting in a way that reflects your desire to be more Christlike, and by being a good steward of your finances.

- Pay up. This is a hard one, but it really takes the message home. There is a story of a parent who returned to his childhood corner store as an adult and gave the long-time owner money that he felt would cover the small things he had stolen as a child. The owner was shocked and impressed with that parent's courage and honesty. Discuss outstanding money issues with your kids. Do they owe money to a friend? Encourage them to clear their slate of unwanted debts.

MOTTO

The only way to be is to live honestly.

JOKE

Why is it dangerous to play cards in Africa?
Because of all the cheetahs.

Tips to Teach It!

Key Verses

Help your children to memorize and understand these verses.

Honesty:

> **"You should want a good name more than you want great riches. To be highly respected is better than having silver or gold." (Proverbs 22:1)**

Integrity:

> **"Those who live without blame walk safely. But those who take crooked paths will get caught." (Proverbs 10:9)**

Key Bible Story

The story of dishonest Gehazi is a great illustration of the importance of being honest with the people in our lives (2 Kings 5).

- Why did Gehazi lie?
- What other things might tempt us to lie?
- What did Gehazi gain by lying?

Teachable Moments

Life situations are the testing ground for honesty and integrity. Use these moments to teach your child these valuable attributes.

Honesty:

- When you catch your children trying to lie, or when they are lied to, discuss the concept of honesty and the consequence of the lie. Talk about how the lie makes you or them feel, and how important it is for you to be able to trust him or her. Teach your child that when we do something wrong, we are better off confessing it right away, rather than lying about it. The consequences will be worse if we lie. Teach your child this law of life: The more you lie, the bigger the problem becomes.

- If your children try to cheat when you are playing a family board game, stop the game and resume it another night when everybody is ready to play fairly and honestly. Explain that cheating leads to bad feelings, and that the Bible says: *"Instead, you yourselves cheat and do wrong. And you do it to your brothers and sisters. Don't you know that evil people will not receive God's kingdom?"* (1 Corinthians 6:8–9).

- If your child plays sports, discuss rules, referees, and the need for honest play. Review some of your child's sports heroes and see where they stand on honesty. If there is a referee clinic or school in your area, encourage your child to learn both sides of their sport—refereeing and playing.

- Children may tell exaggerated stories about each other. They need to be taught that rumors are harmful. Not only do they hurt the wronged individual; they also hurt your reputation as a person of integrity. Teach your children that when they feel tempted to repeat a rumor, they should tell themselves: *"So get rid of every kind of evil. Stop telling lies. Don't pretend to be something you are not. Stop wanting what others have. Don't speak against each other"* (1 Peter 2:1).

TRIVIA

What is the fifth commandment?

"Honor your father and mother."

Integrity:

- If your child wants to buy or rent a video tape, video game, or music CD that is popular, but clearly does not have the type of message you want in your home, talk to him or her about the need to not only believe in a Christian lifestyle, but to live it out. If the child already purchased the item, explain the family rules again, then go with your child to return the item. Talk about how our buying power can vote "yes" for products that express our values, and "no" for products that don't. Tell them that manufacturers listen to our purchasing vote of approval.

- When your children say they are going to do something such as studying, chores, sports, or music practice and they fail to follow through, talk with them about the need to do what they say. Tell your children that people depend on them to follow through on their commitments, and that now is the time to build a good reputation.

- Do your children blame others for problems that they create? Encourage them to be honest in all their dealings. Tell them that if they are willing to take credit for their successes, they should also be willing to take the lumps for their mistakes. Honesty improves every situation. Perhaps you have a story to tell on this issue.

- If your children find a lost item, help them place the article in a safe place so the owner can have it back. This could mean taking it to the store management or placing an ad in the newspaper. Honesty hits home when your children can see the joy of the owner reunited with his treasure.

Tools to Do It!

1 Have your child help you with the restaurant bill to see if it adds up. If the bill is wrong, make sure you have the waitress correct it.

2 Have your child pay for an item and count the change. If the clerk gives you too much or too little, make sure you correct him or her. Honesty in little things says volumes.

3 Catch the mistake. If the viewer is quick they can spot continuity problems in movies and TV. For example, one second an actor is soaking wet and then, in a split second of film time, his shirt is magically dry. Watch a family show or a movie and spot character integrity problems. Talk about when a character isn't being honest or showing integrity. Keep track and see how each dishonest act is resolved or left unresolved by the character. Ask your children the following discussion questions:

- If a character was dishonest, did he or she confess and make things right, or was the dishonesty left uncorrected?

- Do you think the writers and directors forgot to correct it, or did they just not think that it was important?

- What were the consequences to the character's actions?

- This game will lead to some good talk on modern attitudes toward honesty and integrity.

4 Play the "Proverbial Charades Game." Write each of the following Bible verses on separate pieces of paper (all verses taken from the New International Reader's Version). Put the pieces of paper in a hat, bag, or bowl. In teams or individually pick out a verse and do a timed or un-timed charade for the family:

MOTTO

Take an interest in your integrity.

- *"Those who live without blame walk safely. But those who take crooked paths will get caught."* (Proverbs 10:9)

- *"Those who do what is right are guided by their honest lives. But those who aren't faithful are destroyed by their trickery."* (Proverbs 11:3)

- *"The plans of godly people are right. But the advice of sinners will lead you the wrong way."* (Proverbs 12:5)

- *"Those who are honest have respect for the Lord. But those whose paths are crooked hate him."* (Proverbs 14:2)

- *"You should want a good name more than you want great riches. To be highly respected is better than having silver or gold."* (Proverbs 22:1)

- *"It is better to be poor and live without blame than to be rich and follow a crooked path."* (Proverbs 28:6)

- *"Those who hide their sins don't succeed. But those who admit their sins and give them up find mercy."* (Proverbs 28:13)

5 Apply the three R's—Rule, Reason, and Ruler to all that you do.

- **Rule**: The "Do" or "Do Not." For example, tell the truth and be honest in everything you do.

- **Reason**: The reason why keeping the rule makes sense. For example, dishonesty sows distrust and leads to ruined relationships.

- **Ruler**: Behind every rule and reason is God and His character. Take all your explanations back to God and how He made it all to work in line with Himself. For example, God's character and the way He made our world to work is based on honesty. When we follow God's way, things always work better.

Save the Day

Topic

Saving and Planning: What Are They?

Saving is putting aside a planned amount of income each month for a specific purpose. It is an organized system that helps us save enough money to buy expensive items and prepare for future events. Planning is the framework on which we design both our life goals and our financial goals.

Plan to Save, Plan to Succeed

Any discussion of savings plans leaves many people squirming in their designer jeans, but with a few more facts about saving, you can confidently teach your children all they need to know on the subject.

Saving is just delayed spending. Money comes into our lives, and money goes out. That's called "income" and "outgo."

Fail to plan with God, and you are planning to fail. Financial planning gives you the foundation to follow God's leading in your career and personal goals. Financial planning makes all your big and small achievements manageable—whether they be in the fields of education, business, home, retirement, or all the other small things jammed in between.

The first step to solid planning is to find out how God designed finances to work. We need to plan so that some of that outgo gets delayed and can be used to meet future needs. We can use short-term and long-term savings and budgeting to plan for purchases and events in our lives, like college, homes, and car repairs.

Saving and planning allows us to follow God's plan for our lives. It frees us from unnecessary financial stresses that sidetrack us from God's plan. *"The best food and olive oil are stored up in the houses of wise people. But those who are foolish eat up everything they have"* (Proverbs 21:20).

Saving is a godly principle, but, like anything, it has to be used properly. Saving for saving's sake can be as seductive a trap as not saving at all. Money should not be our focus. Focusing on money leads to hoarding. That's not delayed spending—that's delayed living. *"Love for money causes all kinds of evil. Some people want to get rich. They have wandered away from the faith. They have wounded themselves with many sorrows"* (1 Timothy 6:10).

Planning is the framework on which we design our lives and financial goals. God's plan for us is to combine our abilities and finances with His direction to create a lifetime of fulfillment. There will be difficulties, but we can trust that God is with us providing the plan.

JOKE

Where do computers keep their money?

In a memory bank.

When you help your children understand family income, saving, and outgo, you are helping them grasp the value of money. Sure, saving for an item takes longer than using credit, but it teaches valuable life lessons—hard work, sacrifice, informed and time-tempered decisions, patience, and success. These types of lessons can be applied to all areas of life and help build a successful person.

Places to Model It!

In our modern society of computers, cellular phones, and high-tech banking with direct deposits and credit cards, children are sometimes left out of the family money matters loop. Here are some helpful hints on how you can model saving and get your children involved in your adult economics so they know how to handle their own money matters.

Saving:

- Let your children see how money comes into the home, how it is saved, and how it is spent. If that means educating yourself and organizing your money matters a little better, that's a good start.

- Discuss your family's savings goals with your children, and how you plan to achieve those goals. If you want to buy a new television or a nice stereo, pray as a family about the desire and practicality of having that item and about how to develop a savings plan for it. Can you set money aside each month for this item without taking from other savings areas?

Planning:

- Long-term life and financial planning is not strongly emphasized in our society. Planning and saving just doesn't fit into our instant gratification lifestyle. That may be why we find ourselves in instant debt and trouble. Explore your own goals and how you can start now to plan for the future. Sit down with your children and discuss a new family budget, savings goals, and plans for the future. Does the family want to purchase a new car or trailer? Talk about it. Not only does this open the door to questions about money matters; it also gets them excited about what comes next in their lives and how they can prepare for it.

Tips to Teach It!

Key Verses

Help your children memorize and understand these verses.

Saving:

> **"The best food and olive oil are stored up in the houses of wise people. But those who are foolish eat up everything they have." (Proverbs 21:20)**

Planning:

> **"Trust in the Lord with all your heart. Do not depend on your own understanding. In all your ways remember him. Then he will make your paths smooth and straight." (Proverbs 3:5–6)**

Key Bible Story

Saving:

The story of Joseph and his plan to save a nation is a wonderful, exciting story on the victory of planning and saving (Genesis 41).

- How did Joseph make sure Egypt would have food in the future?

- What can you do now to achieve a future goal?

Planning:

Noah's adventure of hearing God, following His plan, and acting it out to achieve victory is one of Genesis' most moving stories (Genesis 6–9).

- What would have happened if he'd tried to build from the middle first?

- What goal can you plan for and then accomplish?

Teachable Moments

Teach your children all about planning and saving through life's little situations and goals. Here are a few suggested opportunities.

Saving:

- When your children are bitten by the impulse-buying bug and want to borrow some money from you to buy an item, teach them the proper savings response. Have them go home and think about the purchase. If they are still eager to get it, have them add it to their savings goals, and then let them return to the store when they've saved enough to purchase it. Loaning money on the spot for impulse buying can set up a pattern of "desire = credit."

• When your child desires to buy or do something special, talk about this desire and pray about it together. Help him or her design a savings plan. This promotes understanding and excitement about setting goals, planning for success, and achieving those goals. Make your child's first savings goals easy to reach. This promotes a sense of accomplishment, incentive, and excitement within a short time.

• If your child sets a goal to buy something like a skateboard, make sure he or she is committed to that goal. If your child wants to switch savings goals in midstream, make sure a lot of research, prayer, and thought go into the change. Have your child compare the benefits of each purchase so he or she isn't disappointed or regretful in the end.

• If your child has selected a rather ambitious savings project like a computer, car, or horseback riding lessons, help with that plan. Suggest that you match his or her savings toward that goal. A dollar-for-dollar arrangement may be a reward for hard work, planning, and commitment.

• If you are about to go on a vacation or a trip but the car breaks down, discuss the options with your children. A simpler vacation might be just as fun, and you can use the extra money to fix the car. Financial planning is about daily choices and how to make the most out of what you have.

Planning:

• If your child wants to have an activity like a picnic or party, help them plan, save, organize, and run the event. These little lessons on planning will add up to a lifetime of successful plans.

• Is your child a young entrepreneur? Help him or her plan and budget for a business. Children can start their own at-home bike repair shop, beverage stand, pet-sitting service, or any number of other businesses.

• Get your children involved in your next family trip from the planning stage to the doing stage. They can plan for their own vacation activities like souvenirs or wind-surfing lessons and then plan to save for them.

- Christmas and other gift-giving events may mean more to your children if they plan and save for a present they can give. Help them with gift ideas or projects that are within their budget. They can plan, budget, save, and then shop or perhaps make their gift. Gift-giving will mean more if they work to get the gift.

Tools to Do It!

Saving:

1 Many banks have fun kid tours, programs, and booklets on saving. Phone ahead for a tour, and see what they have available. They often offer fun stickers or other rewards as incentives.

2 Open a savings account with and for your child.

3 Find out if your bank has a teen program designed to provide information on account options, computer banking, and investment plans. If they do, arrange to have their program representative meet with your teen at the bank to discuss his or her banking needs and questions.

4 Give your children a fun bank or use plastic jars or containers to start them off on the road to saving. Start off with different budgeting categories and give them a family of banks that represent things like tithing (10%), short-term savings (25%), long-term savings (25%), spending (40%).

Planning:

1 Exploring the endless possibilities is often the first step to focusing in on certain career and financial plans. Teens can review their abilities, talents, and interests, then ask themselves some tough questions.

- What does God want me to do? Am I going to university or college?

- What about Bible college?

- Do I want to travel to other countries to do God's work?

- Does starting a business interest me?

- How much money will I need to do what God wants me to do?

2 Make a financial map with your younger children. Start with a simple prayer affirming that God has a plan for each of their lives. What are their interests, abilities, and talents? What do they think God might want them to be when they get older? Let them go crazy with old magazines, newspapers, and art supplies to create a poster with pictures that represent their ideas and dreams. Find pictures to go in the center that illustrate the steps and achievements that would lead to that goal—finishing elementary school, high school, college, saving, part-time jobs, or hobbies. Keep it simple for very young children and help older children explore the subject to make it more complex.

JOKE

What is the only way a miser will swim?

Freestyle.

3 Have your child design and decorate a poster, for his or her study area or your office, with the three important elements of godly career planning:

- God has a plan for you.

- God has given you unique gifts that match His plan for you.

- God will guide and direct you as you pray for His wisdom.

4 Make a Savings Chart. When saving for the big items that your family is looking forward to, like a car, computer, or vacation, get your whole family involved by putting up a savings chart. Tack up a large piece of cardboard and put savings amounts on one half, and time on the other. Indicate the financial goal you must meet to be successful. Chart how much you have saved and how long it has taken you. Discuss how you can increase your savings through earning interest and budgeting. (See chapter 8 for more on budgeting). Make updating the chart a family event. Your children may wish to add some of their budgeted money to the savings goal or start an in-home business to help. Encourage your children to make charts for their own savings goals. These charts are just a way of marking your financial progress, not a basis for running your life.

MOTTO

Plan to be a lifelong saver.

Map It Out

Chapter Eight

Topic

What Is Budgeting?

"Budgeting" is a familiar term to adults. It's simple to make it familiar to children, too. Budgeting is a system that takes our income and divides it into the financial areas of our lives in a manageable, planned, and organized way.

It's Not Really a Scary Part of Life

Never shout "financial budgeting" in a crowded theater—you may start a stampede for the doors. OK, budgeting is not the scary thing it once was. It's just a system that helps us plan what we are going to do with our money, time, and energy.

For many of us, a financial budget is born out of adult necessity or sheer panic, rather than as a result of a lifestyle learned from our parents. Muddled financial organization seems to be a dominant gene in our society. We can break the chain of parental financial illiteracy by teaching our children a system of budgeting their money that can be expanded and enhanced as their financial resources develop and grow. This is the goal of "financial parenting." Open up that mystery called "financial management" and make it as easy and natural as eating or sleeping.

The purpose of a financial budget is to gain control over our outgo so we can have peace of mind and be good stewards. Our goal is to divide our monthly income into age appropriate categories. An adult budget might look like this:

• Tithe 10%	• Taxes 17.5%	• Housing 38%
• Food 12%	• Automobile 15%	• Insurance 5%
• Entertainment/ Recreation 5%	• Clothing 5%	• Debt..................5%
• Savings...........5%	• Medical Expenses ..5%	• Miscellaneous ..5%
• School/ Child Care 8%	• Investments	• Unallocated Surplus

Although at times it can be tedious, gaining control over our finances adds a sense of freedom, confidence, control, and enjoyment to life. Financial stress is often the root of a number of relational and business problems, and can spread to all aspects of our lives.

God's plan is for us to learn a biblically based financial system that will provide for us and give us freedom to obey God. The ideas behind a Christian budget should be to pray, plan, and then follow through with the plan.

Contrary to present opinion, budgeting is not a barrier to our wants—it's the way to achieve our wants. It is the financial gauge that helps us judge our progress towards certain short-term and long-term goals. Budgeting helps us combine short-term and long-term goals into a manageable system of everyday money matters.

Places to Model It!

There are eight important points to biblical budgeting to model to your children.

- Budgeting shows your children that finances and stress do not go hand in hand.

- Budgeting gives you the freedom to follow God's leading and pursue your dreams. You can model this by discussing with your children your special plans for ministries, night school, or other activities, and by telling them how you have saved for these events.

- Budgeting gives you the freedom to buy the things you need or desire. Buying things with cash instead of credit speaks volumes for the importance of a savings plan and savings goals.

- Budgeting frees you from the lure of impulse buying and advertising gimmicks. With a budget you gain control over spending habits and impulses.

- Budgeting gives you the resources for unplanned needs like a sudden illness or car repair.

- Family budgeting changes your children's attitude about money matters. It helps them become aware of the value of a dollar and opens the door to thoughtful money decisions. Get your children involved in your family budget.

MOTTO

A sound budget is smart business.

- You can expand the concept of budgeting from money to other resources to help your family members organize their time, education, careers, and personal growth. Show them how your budget helps you organize your life.

- Budgeting gives your children a clear understanding of God's support, care, and provision for your family. Share stories about times when God's care has been really evident in your family.

Tips to Teach It!

Key Verse

"Suppose someone wants to build a tower. Won't he sit down first and figure out how much it will cost? Then he will see whether he has enough money to finish it. Suppose he starts building and is not able to finish. Then everyone who sees what he has done will laugh at him." (Luke 14:28–29)

Key Bible Story

Read and talk about Gideon's budget (Judges 6–7). God's management of Gideon's army is a lesson in following God's plan.

- Did Gideon need a lot of men to be successful?

- Do we need a lot of money to be successful? No, we just need to know how to use what we have to the fullest, the way God wants us to.

Teachable Moments

To teach your children about a budget you first must have your own budget in order. Getting the family budget together, up-to-date, and working can be a learning experience for the entire family. Take this and other daily opportunities to draw attention to the importance of budgeting.

- When you are working on your own budget and doing the books and your children ask questions, take the time to answer in simple terms so they can understand.

- Get them involved by having them add up a few figures for you in their head or with a calculator.

- They can help look through receipts and staple things together or address and mail envelopes. This provides a family atmosphere for money matters because finances shouldn't feel like a taboo subject.

- The next time you go to the bank or bank machine with your children, make it a special time by letting them push buttons or talk to the clerk. Talk about where the money goes and why. Top off the trip with a treat of some kind.

- When your child is unhappy that certain items are not within his or her or your budget, talk about how overspending in one area means not having enough for other areas.

- When your children want to buy two items but can only afford one, help them examine which item fills their needs most effectively and fits into their budget plan.

- When your children want you to purchase something for them at the store, use the opportunity to explain that it isn't in your budget, but it may be in their budget. Decide together if this item is a need or an impulse buy.

- Encourage your children to budget for and save a little "fun funds" for those unplanned trips to the movies or other fun things. They can select the activity that fits their budget and that would be the most fun.

- *The Giving Bank* (ChariotVictor Publishing) is a great budgeting teaching tool for three- to eight-year-olds.

TRIVIA

Joseph had a 14 year plan to save Egypt.

Tools to Do It!

1 Encourage your children to perform an "Operation Overdrive" as a winter-long savings project. Help your children plan for a fun event like summer soccer school or horse camp. Offer to pay part of the fee if they reach a certain savings goal over the winter.

2 Help your children organize a fund-raising event for their sports team, school, or charity. The event should match the children's age and abilities.

3 Your children can make a priority list for budgeting time as well as money. How much time in a week do your children need for Bible study, family time, homework, chores, sports practice, and fun time? Let them work out a time system for their schedules.

4 Set up a "community tax" box in your home. Parents and children should contribute to it. (See budget suggestions below.) Parents can perhaps match the contributions made by their children. The "tax" money can then be used on an item or activity the family has decided on.

5 Create a budget system or "giving bank" for children ages 3–8. Divide the bank into three categories:

- Giving/Tithing–10%

- Saving–50%

- Spending–40%

For: MISSIONS "FEED THE HUNGRY"

Help your children divide their money into each section by giving them appropriate coins each week. At this age the only thing that should be written down is the savings amount and the price and item for which they are saving.

6 A "mini-budget" for ages 9–12 is essentially the same system as the pre-budget, but with more writing required. Children at this age can use a notebook to approximate a bank book and budget ledger. (See the ledger sheet at the back of this chapter.) A mini-budget consists of four categories (or five if you want them to start paying their community tax):

- Tithing–10%
- Short-term savings–25%
- Long-term savings–25%
- Spending–40%

7 The "teen budget" for ages 13 and up is the stage where your children go to the bank, start their own bank accounts, and learn how the real system works. A teen budget might have these categories:

- Giving–10%
- Community taxes–5%
- Short-term savings–25%
- Long-term savings–25%
- Expenses–10%
- Spending–25%

By this time your teen should be completely familiar with and be able to accomplish all their financial transactions by the same means as adults, be it computer banking or book and ledgers.

8 Make a game of having your children list all the different budget categories they can think of. Have them explain how the categories are connected to each other, and how they help the family, church, or community. Suggested categories and answers are:

- Tithing–10%. Before you spend any of your money, give your tithe to your church.
- Spending–25%. Have a plan and decide what you will spend your money on before you go out.

TRIVIA

How many men out of Gideon's army of 32,000 did God use to fight the Midianites?

300.

- Long-term savings–25%. This is for those big goals you are planning for.

- Short-term savings–25%. This can be used for smaller purchases, like new shoes, videos, or sports gear.

- Taxes–5%. This is much less than you'd have to pay the government, but put it into the family coffers for family activities and savings goals.

- Expenses–10%. That's the cost of living. It could include lessons, community center fees, or your own telephone and bus money. Parents and children should work out those things for which they are financially responsible.

9 *Money Matters for Kids & Teens* has created a number of books, financial systems, and games to help your children plan a budget. Check with your local bookstore.

10 *Larry Burkett's Cash Organizer System* is a great family budgeting tool. It is a four-step system to manage your household income and expenses. It contains:

- Monthly income and expense forms to help you balance your monthly budget.

- Income allocation forms to assist you in distributing your paycheck into your various expense categories.

- An envelope and sticker system that is a handy way to organize expense categories such as housing, food, etc.

- Category ledger sheets to help you keep an organized and manageable running balance on all past transactions and expense categories.

TRIVIA

Where do archaeol-
ogists think the first
coin was made?
*In western Turkey
around 600–640
BC.*

LEDGER

DATE	TRANSACTION	DEPOSIT (+)	WITHDRAWAL (-)	BALANCE

BUDGET TRACKER

DATE	GIVING		COMMUNITY TAXES		EXPENSES		SHORT-TERM SAVINGS		LONG-TERM SAVINGS		SPENDING		TOTAL ALL BALANCES
	TRANSACTION	BALANCE	TRANSACTION	BALANCE	TRANSACTION	BALANCE	TRANSACTION	BALANCE	TRANSACTION	BALANCE	TRANSACTION	BALANCE	

In the *transaction* column, write where the money came from or where it is going. In the *balance* column, write the new total.

Spending Spree

Topic

What Is Spending?

Children already know about spending. The goal is to train them to spend wisely. Spending is simply the "outgo" of your "income." Smart spending is using your budgeted money wisely (by comparison shopping and research) to get the best value for your money and time.

Spending—Part of Our Daily Lives

Lessons in smart spending are essential in our consumer-driven culture. The following consumer suggestions will make your child a savvy shopper:

Understanding where and how our money should go out of our lives is the point of godly spending. Spending is not about draining our resources to the point of exhaustion or total financial collapse. Spending is a system of planned, saved, budgeted, and researched purchases.

When we shop, we should be exhausting our feet, not our finances. How we handle our spending affects both our present and future quality of life. Over spending today leads to "over-your-head-debt" tomorrow. *"He spent everything he had. Then the whole country ran low on food. So the son didn't have what he needed"* (Luke 15:14).

A financial budget is the tool that helps us plan, manage, control, and provide goals for our spending habits. Here are some good reasons for spending: to provide for daily necessities; to experience different things and enjoy life; to educate ourselves or start a business; to acknowledge God by giving Him our firstfruits or tithe.

When we budget and prioritize our spending needs, we are being good stewards of God's resources. Spending within our means, with a plan, spares us the stress, uncertainty, and other negative consequences that come with debt. Planned spending allows us to slow down and get what we need, when we need it, for a good value.

Charity spending is an often over-looked aspect of spending. It tends to get overshadowed by product spending. Charity spending, as with any spending venture, must be planned, budgeted, and researched. Find out all you can about the charities to which you give money. Be a charity shopper by selecting causes that interest you and organizations that are reputable, do what they say, and practice wise financial stewardship.

TRIVIA

How much do teenagers spend a year in the US? *Well over 28.5 million dollars.*

Places to Model It!

Smart shopping is a pattern of consumer awareness that you can teach, model, and succeed in. Remember, your children are watching and following your lead. The act of spending money is never easy. It is fraught with temptation, advertising sensory overload, and good and bad products or "deals." Here are a few spending tips:

MOTTO

Smart shoppers avoid bad buys.

- Shop around for an item while you're still saving for it. Your children will see that you are trying to find the best value for your dollar.

- Pray for consumer wisdom. Your children should see you asking your heavenly Father for financial advice.

- Before shopping, make a list. Buy only the items from the list.

- Give yourself a spending limit, and if a purchase is over that limit go home and think about it for at least 24 hours.

- Let your children see how you research for the best time to get a deal, like purchasing playground equipment in the winter.

- Demonstrate wise shopping by never shopping when you are hungry, stressed, or tired. Go shopping only when you are mentally ready to do some focused, controlled, consumer snooping.

- Demonstrate a keen eye for warranty and return policies. Show your children how you get the best value for your money.

- Don't shop with a friend who is known for impulse shopping.

- Don't buy when pressured to by seductive sales, aggressive clerks, or advertising lures.

- Take some "fun funds" for small treats after a successful shopping mission.

77

- At the end of the shopping trip thank God for His provision.

- Let your children see you following these time-honored consumer tips for getting the best value for your dollar:

  - Listen closely to what advertisers are actually saying about a product.

  - Don't be dazzled by media glitz.

  - Compare products. Explore different brand names.

  - Shop around. Don't just go where the commercials tell you to go.

  - Go for quality. Make sure the product lives up to its advertiser's claim. Check out the relevant consumer reports. It may be worth paying more for a product that will last longer or has a better warranty. Balance it out.

  - Look past the appeal of products that make you look good or feel cool to what you really need.

Tips to Teach It!

Key Verse

"He spent everything he had. Then the whole country ran low on food. So the son didn't have what he needed." **(Luke 15:14)**

Key Bible Story

The parable of the lost son or "the son who spent like there was no tomorrow" is an easy story for children to understand (Luke 15:11–32). Encourage discussion by asking:

- Was the lost son a wise spender?

- What was the result of his spending habits?

- How can you avoid his mistake?

Teachable Moments

Spending is a daily event in most of our lives, so there are hundreds of opportunities in your week to teach good shopping habits.

- When your child has saved for a designer product, help him or her to be a wise consumer and get value for his or her dollar. Help your children research and purchase quality products by teaching them these "value-able" shopping tips:

  - Make your purchase when you need it.

  - Buy it for a good price.

  - Buy products from reliable companies with fair return or warranty policies.

  - Make an informed purchase by avoiding advertising gimmicks, impulse buying, and high-pressure sales tactics.

  - Don't circumvent the globe to find your buy. Your time and gas driving across town is probably worth more than the two dollars you saved at the "across-town" sale.

- When shopping, help your children compare brand names. Discuss your findings and see if the pros and cons outweigh the status of the brand name. Compare the price difference between brands and explore what other uses they could find for the money they would save by buying the less expensive brand. If they decide the brand name image or quality warrants the extra money, and they are prepared to use their own money, let them make that choice.

- When exploring brands and companies, help your children understand that the philosophy of a company should matter to them just as much as the product they produce. As part of their product research, have your children do some detective work:

  - Write a letter to the company asking about the company's ethical policies.

  - Search the Internet for the company's mission statement or philosophies.

  - Find out about the company through articles and news stories.

  - If, in the end, the company does not stand up to their testing, they can write the president of the company and explain why they don't agree with the company's policies, and why they chose another brand. Even young people can make a difference with their purchasing power.

- In the grocery store, compare prices on various product sizes. Take a calculator to figure the price per unit, and compare values.

- If your children want to get involved when you purchase a big family item like a car, let them. Give them consumer books to explore makes and models. Post a list of criteria you are looking for in a car, such as passenger capacity, intended uses, age of the vehicle, price range, color, style, and make. Your children will have a great time circling ads, surfing the Internet, or hunting through the library for consumer information that fits the bill. This makes spending a family event and helps your children get involved in the planning and excitement of finding that special item.

Tools to Do It!

1 Have your children research the future costs, maintenance, and commitment to such purchases as sports equipment, pets, or cars. Have them make a product research scrapbook. It can include pictures,

drawings, and information on that item. If your children want to buy a pet, such as a fish, their book would include the following information:

- Different types of fish and their care

- Aquarium and equipment costs and types

- Monthly food, chemical, and gravel costs

Understanding the future financial commitments to things they own now is something that your children will use over and over. It will help them avoid impulse buys.

2 Play "Shop for a Day" by giving your children thirty dollars and asking them to plan and then buy one day's worth of groceries. Let them plan their menu and then go with them to the store. This is a great lesson in practical daily shopping. The rules to this activity are:

- They only need to buy the main food items. Condiments and spices are provided.

- They must provide the ingredients for three sit-down meals.

- They must be normal meals that your family will eat.

- Fruit, meat, vegetables, breads, and dairy products must be in the plan.

If they meet all the rest of the above requirements, they can buy any dessert they want with the remaining money.

3 When your child has been dreaming of that special item like a baseball glove, a car, a dog, or a special dress, and you're sure it's a genuine and consistent desire, step in and help him or her properly plan for that purchase. Help work the item into his or her savings plan. Do some research or comparison snooping together. Make an outing of shopping with them and comparing brand names, store policies, and company warranties. Walking through the process of

smart shopping makes your children confident, informed, and satisfied shoppers.

4. When your child is planning a purchase, have them copy and answer this checklist for a good deal.

- Compared to other products, is this item low, average, or highly priced?

- Compared to other products, is this item well-made, with quality materials?

- Does this product have a good warranty?

- Is this product exactly what you were looking for? If not, why not? Are you compromising what you really want?

- Does the manufacturer have a good reputation?

- Does the store or manufacturer have a good return policy?

Several consumer research options are available. These include the newspaper, store flyers or advertisements, the Better Business Bureau, the library, consumer guides, special interest clubs, and the Internet.

TRIVIA

How much do teens spend at the mall each trip?

Between $10 and $50.

To Your Credit

Chapter Ten

Topic

Credit and Debt: What Are They?

Credit is easily available everywhere today. For that reason, it is important to teach our children that credit is money that is borrowed for a specific purpose and then repaid right away. Debt is not having enough money to carry out our daily financial obligations—whether living expenses or loan payments.

Credit and Debt Are Not the Same Thing!

Contrary to popular rumor, credit is not the evil brother of saving. Credit is a financial tool just like any other. The problem comes when we misuse the credit system, because misuse leads to debt. We can successfully teach our children the difference between credit and debt.

In the Bible, God gave us a system of money management that will keep us out of debt. First, we need to seek God and trust His Word. Second, we must seek godly council from people with financial experience. And third, we should apply biblical stewardship to our finances. Everything in our financial arsenal, from credit use to investments, must have a godly foundation if it is to work properly.

God's system is based on the following philosophy: plan now, save for the future, and buy when ready. Unfortunately, the modern standard is "Buy now, save later, and hope you have the cash in the future." We need to return to the basic godly principles of hard work, contentment, godly stewardship, and sound financial planning.

Credit should not and does not always lead to debt. The most common use of credit today is through a pre-approved line of credit (credit cards). This system is used to purchase items without using cash. But it comes with a high interest rate. It is a great credit system if we have saved the money to back up our spending, and, therefore, don't pay interest. But when we use credit with no savings support, we are borrowing money that we do not have the resources to repay, and then paying interest on top of it.

When credit is used responsibly, in conjunction with budgeting and saving, it is a very useful money tool. In fact, a good credit rating speaks for our responsibility, and our business and financial management skills. It can encourage business relations and financial trust. The following are some credit safety tips:

- Back your credit use with money you have saved already.

QUOTE

A wise man builds his house upon a rock. A foolish man builds his house on sand (Matthew 7:24–27).

- Pay all your credit card bills completely each and every month. The first time you can't pay off your credit bills, stop using credit.

- Use your credit as a tool to enhance your money management, not increase your spending power. Never use credit as a replacement for money you don't have. Only spend money on things you have budgeted for. Never extend your credit past what your income can afford.

- Misuse of credit means paying interest, while saving is earning you interest. Which system is working *for* you?

- Over-borrowing is a burden that seems to be crippling us as a nation, and debt is the nasty little reward. Remember, wrongful financial obligation can be a barrier to doing the things God wants us to do, while budgeting and saving gives us financial freedom. *"Rich people rule over those who are poor. Borrowers are slaves to lenders"* (Proverbs 22:7).

Places to Model It!

The young age range that credit card companies start marketing to is amazing. Teens are wandering around with personal lines of credit, but have no idea of the consequences of misuse and no resources to pay for mistakes. Consequently, your children are never too young to start learning proper credit use. Here are a few ways to be a positive financial example at home.

Dealing with Debt:
- If you are already in debt, use this rather uncomfortable position to teach one huge lesson. Tell your children that money is a problem right now, but that you have learned a few things and, as a family, you are going to focus on getting out of debt. Perhaps kick off your new

"Financial Olympic Games" with a credit card cutting ceremony. Make a plan for getting out of debt, and get the entire family involved. This could mean discussing impulse buying, downsizing family entertainment plans, or just setting up a "debt fund," where family members can deposit coins into a jar to go towards debt reduction.

- With a positive attitude and an eye to celebrate little successes, let your children see the family work their way out of debt. Remember, you can be just as creative about getting out of debt as you were getting into it. Your victory over your debt can be the starting point for a knowledgeable, manageable, and godly financial life for your children.

JOKE

What happens if you trip on your pile of IOUs?

You fall into debt.

Teaching Godly Finances:

- Don't teach your children the debt road by loaning them money they don't have, or giving them advances on their allowances. Model the concept of delayed gratification.

Using Credit:

- If you use credit cards, always remember to explain to your children that you aren't using them because you don't have money. Explain to them that the money is already in the bank. The card is just more convenient at times, and is useful for prudent record keeping.

- Show them how some credit card companies give you a percentage back for purchases or for paying off your balance on time.

- Make sure your children understand that all your purchases are planned purchases. Let them see you paying the bill as soon as it comes in.

Smart Budgeting:

- Let your children help you with your budget so that they can see how you allocate expenses. By watching you successfully budget, your children will have the knowledge and confidence to do the same with their money—now and later.

Tips to Teach It!

Key Verse

Help your children memorize and understand these verses.

Credit:

> **"Rich people rule over those who are poor. Borrowers are slaves to lenders."**
> **(Proverbs 22:7)**

Debt:

> **"Pay everything you owe. But you can never pay back all the love you owe each other. Those who love others have done everything the law requires."**
> **(Romans 13:8)**

Key Bible Stories

Credit:

The story of the widow's oil is about trusting God in both good and bad financial times (2 Kings 4:1–7).

- Do you think it was easy for the widow to trust Elisha?

- What's an area in your life that you can trust God for?

Debt:

The parable of the unmerciful servant tells about God's mercy to us and our responsibility to do the same for others (Matthew 18:21–35).

- What do you think the unmerciful servant thought was more important, people or money?

- What's most important to you?

Teachable Moments

It's important for young children to learn how to handle all their money tools, including credit. Understanding how credit works in situations now will help them when they become adults. Use these everyday events to teach on-the-go money matters.

Credit:

* When your children want to make a large purchase that you feel might strap their finances, help them to consider that the absence of the money might mean God doesn't want them to have the item. Pray about it together. If the item is important, and urgently needed, God may want you to buy it as a gift instead of getting into the trap of loaning them money.

* Perhaps your child has already loaned money to a friend and now the friend isn't paying it back. Talk to your child about what we should value more: the people in our lives or our money. The solution might be to forget about the debt and not loan to that friend in the future.

* If your teen is preparing to buy a car, never co-sign a loan for him or her. That just gets them in debt! Better financial choices are:

    – They can save for the car. It takes longer but the rewards are deeper.

    – You might match their savings for that goal.

    – Help them shop around for a car that is within his or her means.

Debt:

* If you are in the habit of lending your children money for purchases and taking it out of their allowance later, you are modeling a debt lifestyle. Here are a few alternative ideas:

    – Have them wait, save, and return for that item another day.

- Use a prior system of credit (more on this later).

- Buy the item for them as a gift, if it fits into your budget.

- Use the store's layaway plan, if it has one.

• If your children borrow money from a friend, make sure they repay that friend immediately. They should only do this when they have the money in the bank and the item is budgeted for.

MOTTO

Don't make a date

with debt.

Tools to Do It!

1 Set up a system of credit with your children based on the savings they already have. If they want to purchase an item but don't have the cash, they can call upon this prearranged credit up to the amount they have in their savings. When they get home they must pay you promptly. This credit does not extend over times when they do not have savings in their account. The *Larry the Cat Debit Card* at the end of this chapter can be photocopied and carried in a wallet or purse. When they use it, the card is given to you, and when they pay you back, the card is returned to them.

2 Go with your older children or teens to the bank and help them get a debit card for their savings accounts. Explain in detail that when they use the debit card, they are using money they already have saved and it comes directly out of their account.

3 After your teens have properly managed all the elements of a teen budget for a period of time, it may be time to introduce them to their own credit cards. Write down a set of rules that both sides agree to and will follow. For example:

• Use the credit card only for budgeted items.

- Pay the balance off at the end of each month.

- Cut up the card the first time it's not paid off.

It's better to teach and watch them while they are in your home than for them to learn the hard way once they are out on their own.

4. Use a home banking/checking system for your children. Photocopy the checks and ledger forms at the end of this chapter or create your own personal designer checks. Your children can set up a checking account with you. They can deposit money each week or month into a home account with you, and take their checkbook and ledger with them to the store. Instead of cash, they write you a check for their purchases, then they write the amount in the ledger to keep track of their account balance. You do

JOKE

What's the best
thing to do when an
elephant charges
you?
Pay him!

the same in your parent ledger, then you take their check, give them the money or pay for the item, remove the amount from their account, stamp the check, and give it back to them. Reconcile your ledgers together at the end of each month.

5 Make a family scrapbook entitled "Down on Debt." Get a large inexpensive scrapbook and art supplies and fill the book with debt-related information such as:

- Bible verses concerning debt

- Newspaper articles on debt

- Quotes and photocopies from this and other financial books and articles

- Magazine and newspaper ads that promote purchasing with credit with no mention of saving

- Family stories, or ones from friends, telling how they got out of debt, or how making no-debt choices benefitted them

- At the end of the book have a page entitled "Soldiers Against Debt." Glue in a picture of the family and include their signatures around the borders

6 Play *Larry Burkett's Money Matters* board game (ages 12–adult), or *Money Matters for Kids* board game (ages 3–8). It makes learning about money matters fun and educational.

TRIVIA

How did Joseph prepare Egypt for the famine?
He had people save food for seven years (Genesis 41:34).

BLANK CHECKS

CHECK #_____

DATE_____

PAY TO THE
ORDER OF_____ $_____

_____DOLLARS

SIGNATURE_____

CHECK #_____

DATE_____

PAY TO THE
ORDER OF_____ $_____

_____DOLLARS

SIGNATURE_____

CHECK #_____

DATE_____

PAY TO THE
ORDER OF_____ $_____

_____DOLLARS

SIGNATURE_____

CHECK REGISTER

DATE	TRANSACTION	DEPOSIT (+)		WITHDRAWAL (-)		BALANCE	

Business by the Book

Chapter Eleven

Topic

What Is Business?

If your children have entrepreneurial interests, they'll need to know the basics of godly business practices. Business is the buying and selling of products and/or services. Good business sense is a strong knowledge of all the details that go into running or participating in a business, and being aware of new business opportunities.

Business Is an Important Part of Our Lives

The creation of different businesses, no matter what they might be, is the backbone of our society. To help your children understand the endless opportunities that lay ahead, they need to understand the basic facts of business.

Honor God. The business you do and the way in which you do it should reflect God's presence in your life. As a Christian, your first step in business or career planning is to bring everything to God in prayer. Make sure your business reflects God's principles and value system.

Keep the customer happy. Big or small, the manufacturing and distribution of services or products, and the relationship between seller and buyer, are always balancing acts between business profit and consumer buying power. To work effectively, both sides have to be satisfied with the outcome of the exchange of goods or services for money.

Excellence always. Doing things with excellence, treating customers well, and pricing fairly will build a strong business and a good reputation.

Work smarter and harder. We can do this by increasing the value of our working hour through learned skills, or by increasing our efficiency. These two factors together enhance our business or career value. Money, as we know it today, is the predominant means of measuring and assigning value to our skills, time, and products. We need to understand how to make that monetary value work for us now and in the future.

Charge appropriate prices. Consumers want quality products and services that they can afford, while a business must meet certain financial obligations to succeed. These obligations include the manufacture of a product or service, production of enough of a product or service to establish a market with a fair price, advertising, delivery of the product, competitiveness, repayment of investors or creditors, and, if God leads that way, expansion. Consumer demand for a decent product, competition, and a company's ability to answer its financial obligations determine if a company is a success or not.

Business offers another important service to the community: It employs individuals, who in turn become consumers and purchase from other businesses.

Places to Model It!

Introducing your children to business doesn't mean a complicated walk down Wall Street, complete with profit graphs and accountants. Helping your children see the endless possibilities in business or the benefits of employee initiative will help them be successful. These initiatives work for their own entrepreneurial explorations and also at school and on the job. Always in the forefront of these learning times should be the knowledge that God is here with a plan and wants to help direct us in our quest for employment or business.

- Be an entrepreneur yourself. Have an eye out for business opportunities for you and your children. Do this by helping your children set up their own at-home business or let them help you set up yours. Go with them on a snowy day and shovel walks for money, return bottles for the deposit, or make crafts together for the Christmas craft fair.

- Get the job done. When planning jobs at home, like doing your own remodeling, repairing, or decorating, go about it like you are doing a business. Teach your children about planning, researching, budgeting, supply purchasing, time budgeting, quality work, and right work attitudes right in your own home.

- Demonstrate good business ethics. Be an outstanding employee or business owner that goes the extra mile beyond what is expected. Teach

excellence. When you get letters, rewards, or promotions for a job well done, tell your kids so they can see the rewards of diligence.

- Be a good Christian witness. Through your experiences your children will see the proper Christian response to daily career situations. Be a witness in your career for both your colleagues and your family. Christian ethics in business is the most important career lesson of all. *"Work at everything you do with all your heart. Work as if you were working for the Lord, not for human masters"* (Colossians 3:23).

Tips to Teach It!

Key Verse

"Don't do anything only to get ahead. Don't do it because you are proud. Instead, be free of pride. Think of others as better than yourselves. None of you should look out just for your own good. You should also look out for the good of others." (Philippians 2:3–4)

Key Bible Story

The silversmiths who could not hear God's message because of greed is a profound New Testament story that teaches us to honor God above our business lives (Acts 19:24–41).

- These people were angry with Paul because their priorities were wrong. What was their priority?

- What is your first priority?

Teachable Moments

Many everyday situations can help you illustrate the concept of business to your children. The following points are just a few suggestions to help you recognize teachable moments:

- When your older child has an interest in a career or business, help him or her arrange a tour, an interview, or perhaps a volunteer position related to their interest.

- When you are in a business (hairdresser, sports store, etc.) evaluate it with your children. Does it seem prosperous and successful? Why or why not?

- When your children want to earn extra money, help them find home business opportunities that fit their age, abilities, and interests. Teach them how to do the job right by showing them how to:

    – Plan a business.

    – Budget and cost out their service or product.

    – Buy materials.

    – Produce their service or product.

    – Advertise their product or service.

    – Conduct their business.

    If that means doing it with them, then take time out to be a business consultant.

    Explain to your children that making a good product or performing a good service and treating a customer right build a good reputation every time and everywhere we work.

JOKE

Where's the best place to build offices for optometrists? *On a site for sore eyes.*

- When your children sign on for a job, be it for work, school, or charity events, and discover it isn't what they wanted or expected, help them find the motivation, commitment, and ideas to do a great job anyway.

- A good starter book for children is *50 Money Making Ideas for Kids* (Tommy Nelson, 1997). The right attitude in small business leads to the right attitude in life business.

JOKE

What did the ski instructor say to his actor student?

There's no business like snow business.

Tools to Do It!

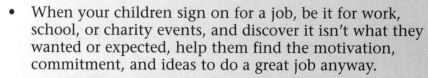

1 On the days when your children ask you how work was, tell them about your day. Together you can enjoy your successes and discuss problem-solving for bad days. Ask your children how their day was, too. Compare the differences and similarities.

2 Take your child to work with you when you can. Show him or her what you do, what the business does, and how it works. Help your child see how the pieces and people fit together. Let your child see business both as an individual entity, and as part of the community.

3 Go to the library and check out books on careers and entrepreneurs, or surf the Internet with your children. Discuss the stories you find.

4 Help your child make a list of his or her talents and of careers that might use those abilities.

5 Get a personality test or go together with your child to get tested. Take your results and discuss how they can help you and your child with your education, career, and volunteer planning. Try *The PathFinder* (Personality Analysis) by Christian Financial Concepts.

6 Help your child pull together a winning résumé that is sharp, easy-to-read, and informative. Browse some résumé books or

computer programs to find the right one. Make
sure the résumé includes brief statements about:

- Personal accomplishments, like the honor
  roll or sports awards.

- Job experience.

- Personal abilities and talents that make
  your child an asset.

- Letters of references from teachers,
  employers, or coaches.

7 Do a mock job interview
with your children tohelp
them prepare for the real
thing. Go over what went
well and what should be
changed.

8 Encourage your teen to
research potential employers
and companies by searching
the Internet, asking past
employees about their work
experience, reading articles,
or asking the company for a mission statement.
Help your child find an employer that practices
ethics and honesty in business.

9 If your child has invented an interesting game or
product, walk him or her through the process of
copyright and marketing. Perhaps your child can
get involved in a young entrepreneur organization.

10 Sit down and discuss what indications your
children have found in their career planning
that God is in it and directing them. Pray with
them for God's continuing grace and direction.

11 Encourage your teen to
explore volunteer opportunities. In the process your
child can:

- Help out an organization.
- Learn new things.
- Have great experiences.
- Get some good references.
- Learn to make more informed
  career and education decisions
  later.

What Really Matters

What Really Matters

Money Matters

By now you've seen how any experience in life can be used as a teaching opportunity. And, since money matters impact almost every aspect of our lives, the opportunities are endless. When you started this book, it may have seemed a daunting task to teach your children about godly stewardship and money matters. But once you start pulling apart the different pieces of stewardship and using those teachable moments that life provides, it isn't that difficult.

You now have the necessary teaching tools to teach money matters to your children, and you have developed an eye to

recognize the opportunities to teach your children the concepts of everyday, godly financial decisions. Wherever you are, whether it is facing those unexpected financial needs like car repairs, giving to the needy, planning for the future, or just browsing in the mall, you can do it the way God wants. Behind all your understanding of stewardship, finances, and training your children is the knowledge that God enjoys providing for all of their needs. This includes providing opportunities to teach your children when they will be most receptive. With thankful hearts, you can share His wisdom with your children as life supplies the lessons.

As you teach in the middle of life, your children will learn, practice, and explore in a safe, mentored, and modeled environment. As they mature, so should their independence and exploration of the world of finance. You can be confident that you have passed down to them the training, knowledge, tools, and opportunities that will enable them to be financially independent.

God Matters

God is the greatest economist. He knows how life works best. When we help our children understand this important fact, we are teaching them how to live and work in the world the way God wants them to. Underlying all the teaching that leads our children down the road of financial independence is this understanding that our personal money matters are dependent on God. God, His love, and His Word should rule every aspect of our life and finances—from our attitudes and careers, to our social interactions, to our savings accounts. We accomplish this through teaching and applying godly principles to events and situations in the middle of life. *"The commandments I give you today must be in your hearts. Make sure your children learn them. Talk about them when you are at home. Talk about them when you walk along the road. Speak about them when you go to bed. And speak about them when you get up"* (Deuteronomy 6:6–7).

What Really Matters

Making you the perfect financial parent is not the object of this book. What matters is that you teach in a warm and loving environment—mistakes and all. Remember, money and finances are just tools we use every day. How we handle them is about how we handle ourselves.

Our relationships with God and our children are what matter most. When we confidently live out these relationships in the midst of the frantic pace of life, all of life's lessons come a little easier.

This book has provided the basic tools. Now it's just a matter of going out and using those daily teachable moments!

Additional Resources

Books

Burkett, Larry. *The Financial Planning Organizer*. Chicago, IL: Moody 1991.

———. *The Financial Planning Workbook*. Chicago, IL: Moody Press, 1990.

———. *Money Management for College Students*. Chicago, IL: Moody, 1998.

Burkett, Larry and Rick Osborne. *Financial Parenting*. Chicago, IL: Moody, 1999.

———. *Your Child Wonderfully Made*. Chicago, IL: Moody, 1998.

Burkett, Larry with Ed Strauss. *Buying Your First Car*. Chicago, IL: Moody, 2000.

———. *Getting Your First Credit Card*. Chicago, IL: Moody, 2000.

———. *Renting Your First Apartment*. Chicago, IL: Moody, 2000.

Burkett, Larry with K. Christie Bowler. *A Different Kind of Party*. Chicago, IL: Moody, 2000 (Ages 6–10).

———. *A Home for the Hamsters*. Chicago, IL: Moody, 2000 (Ages 6–10).

———. *Last Chance for Camp*. Chicago, IL: Moody, 2000 (Ages 6–10).

———. *Sarah and the Art Contest*. Chicago, IL: Moody, 2000 (Ages 6–10).

Burkett, Larry with Kevin Miller. *Preparing for College*. Chicago, IL: Moody, 2000.

Burkett, Larry with Todd Temple. *Money Matters for Teens Workbooks (Ages 11–14 & 15–18 Editions)*. Chicago, IL: Moody, 1998.

Ellis, Lee. *The PathFinder: A Guide to Career Decision Making*. Christian Financial Concepts, 1995.

50 Money Making Ideas for Kids. Nashville, TN: Tommy Nelson, 1997.

Home Allowance and Chore Kit. Colorado Springs, CO: ChariotVictor, 2000.

Job Board. Colorado Springs, CO: ChariotVictor, 2000.

Lucas, Daryl J., ed. *105 Questions Children Ask About Money Matters*. Wheaton, IL: Tyndale, 1997.

Money Matters for Kids. Chicago, IL: Moody, available February 2001.

Money Matters for Teens. Chicago, IL: Moody, available February 2001.

One Big House. Compassion International Publications.

Sande, Corlette. *The Young Peacemaker*. Billings, MT: Peacemaker Ministries, 1996.

Weidmann, Jim and Kurt Bruner, with L. Allen Burkett. *Money Matters Family Nights*. Colorado Springs, CO: ChariotVictor, 1998.

Games and Resources

Larry Burkett's Money Matters Game. Colorado Springs, CO: Rainfall, 1996.

Money Matters for Kids Game. Colorado Springs, CO: Rainfall, 1998.

My Giving Bank. Colorado Springs, CO: ChariotVictor, 1996.

Web Sites

Christian Financial Concepts: www.cfcministry.org

Lightwave Publishing: www.lightwavepublishing.com

Money Matters for Kids: www.mm4kids.org

Start Your Own Business: www.treas.gov/kids/kidsmoney.html

US Patent & Trademark Office: www.uspto.gov

Lightwave's Resource Products

For Kids and Teens

Lambier, Doug and Robert Stevenson. *Genesis for Kids*. Nashville, TN: Tommy Nelson, 1997 (ages 8–14).

Lightwave Creative Team. *The Amazing Treasure Bible Storybook*. Grand Rapids, MI: Zondervan, 1997 (ages 8–12).

Osborne, Rick and K. Christie Bowler. *I Want to Know About the Bible*. Grand Rapids, MI: Zondervan, 1998 (ages 8–12).

———. *I Want to Know About God*. Grand Rapids, MI: Zondervan, 1998 (ages 8–12).

———. *I Want to Know About Jesus*. Grand Rapids, MI: Zondervan, 1998 (ages 8–12).

———. *I Want to Know About Prayer*. Grand Rapids, MI: Zondervan, 1998 (ages 8–12).

———. *I Want to Know About the Church*. Grand Rapids, MI: Zondervan, 1998 (ages 8–12).

———. *I Want to Know About the Holy Spirit*. Grand Rapids, MI: Zondervan, 1998 (ages 8–12).

———. *I Want to Know About the Ten Commandments*. Grand Rapids, MI: Zondervan, 1998 (ages 8–12).

———. *I Want to Know About the Fruit of the Spirit*. Grand Rapids, MI: Zondervan, 1999 (ages 8–12).

Osborne, Rick and Elaine. *The Singing Bible (Audio Tape Set)*. Wheaton, IL: Tyndale, 2000 (ages 4–10).

van der Maas, Ed M. *Adventure Bible Handbook*. Grand Rapids, MI: Zondervan, 1994 (ages 8–12).

For Parents

Bowman, Crystal and Tricia Goyer. *Mealtime Moments* Wheaton, IL: Tyndale, 2000.

Dall, Jeanette, Carla Williams and B. J. Bassett. *My Time With God*. Wheaton, IL: Tyndale, 2000.

KidCordance. Grand Rapids, MI: Zondervan, 1999.

Lederman, Jacqueline. *Joy Ride!* Wheaton, IL: Tyndale, 2000.

The NIrV Kids' Quest Study Bible. Grand Rapids, MI: Zondervan, 1998.

Osborne, Rick. *Teaching Your Child How to Pray*. Chicago, IL: Moody, 2000.

———. *Talking to Your Children About God*. New York: Harper San Francisco, 1998.

Osborne, Rick with K. Christie Bowler. *Your Child and the Christian Life*. Chicago, IL: Moody, 1998.

Osborne, Rick with Kevin Miller. *Your Child and the Bible*. Chicago, IL: Moody, 1998.

———. *Your Child and Jesus*. Chicago, IL: Moody, 1999.

Rice, Wayne and David R. Veerman. *Reality 101*. Wheaton, IL: Tyndale, 1992.

Trent, John, Rick Osborne, and Kurt Bruner, gen. eds. *Parents' Guide to the Spiritual Growth of Children*. Wheaton, IL: Tyndale, 2000.

Veerman, David R., et al. *101 Questions Children Ask About God*. Wheaton, IL: Tyndale, 1992.

———. *102 Questions Children Ask About the Bible*. Wheaton, IL: Tyndale, 1994.

———. *103 Questions Children Ask About Right from Wrong*. Wheaton, IL: Tyndale, 1995.

———. *104 Questions Children Ask About Heaven and Angels*. Wheaton, IL: Tyndale, 1996.

———. *106 Questions Children Ask About Our World*. Wheaton, IL: Tyndale, 1998.

———. *107 Questions Children Ask About Prayer*. Wheaton, IL: Tyndale, 1998.

———. *108 Questions Children Ask About Friends & School*. Wheaton, IL: Tyndale, 1999.

———. *801 Questions Children Ask About God*. Wheaton, IL: Tyndale, 2000.

Games

The Book Game. Wheaton, IL: Tyndale, 1999 (ages 5 to adult).

House Rules. Wheaton, IL: Tyndale, 1999 (ages 5 to adult).

Sticky Situations. Wheaton, IL: Tyndale, 1991 (ages 6 to adult).

What Would Jesus Do?. Wheaton, IL: Tyndale, 1998 (ages 6 to adult).

Web Site

Lightwave Publishing:
www.lightwavepublishing.com

Money Matters for Kids™ **& Teens** is providing tips and tools children need to understand the biblical principles of stewardship. Money Matters for Kids is committed to see the next generation grounded in God's Word and living His principles.

Money Matters for Kids and Teens materials are adapted by **Lightwave Publishing** from the works of best-selling author on business and personal finances, **Larry Burkett**. Larry is the founder and president of **Christian Financial Concepts**™, author of more than 60 books, and hosts a radio program aired on more than 1,000 outlets worldwide. Money Matters for Kids has a fun kids' and teens' Web site, along with a special Money Matters Parenting Resource section.

Visit Money Matters for Kids Web site at: **www.mm4kids.org**

building Christian faith in families

Lightwave Publishing is one of North America's leading developers of quality resources that encourage, assist, and equip parents to build Christian faith in their families. Their products help parents answer their children's questions about the Christian faith, teach them how to make church, Sunday school, and Bible reading more meaningful for their children, provide them with pointers on teaching their children to pray, and much, much more.

Lightwave, together with its various publishing and ministry partners, such as Focus on the Family, has been successfully producing innovative books, music, and games for the past 15 years. Some of their more recent products include the *Parents' Guide to the Spiritual Growth of Children, Mealtime Moments, Joy Ride!* and *My Time With God*.

Lightwave also has a fun kids' web site and an Internet-based newsletter called *Tips and Tools for Spiritual Parenting*. For more information and a complete list of Lightwave products, please visit: **www.lightwavepublishing.com.**

MOODY
The Name You Can Trust
A MINISTRY OF MOODY BIBLE INSTITUTE

Moody Press, a ministry of Moody Bible Institute, is designed for education, evangelization, and edification.

If we may assist you in knowing more about Christ and the Christian life, please write us without obligation:

Moody Press, c/o MLM
Chicago, IL 60610

Or visit us at Moody's Web site: **www.moodypress.org**

Follow God

Openly seek God in all things (Philippians 3:14).

Love One Another

Strive for mutual love and respect (1 John 3:23).

Love Yourself

Love and care for yourself (Philippians 4:8; 1 Peter 3:3–4).

Choose God

Submit your will to God's will and make right choices (Matthew 16:24–25).

The Meter is Running

Manage your time wisely (Matthew 25:1–13).

Handle With Care

Be responsible and generous with your possessions (2 Corinthians 9:6–8).

Just Do It (for God)

Use your gifts and talents for God (Romans 12:1–8)